MULTILINGUAL WRITERS AND WRITING CENTERS

MULTILINGUAL WRITERS AND WRITING CENTERS

BEN RAFOTH

UTAH STATE UNIVERSITY PRESS
Logan

© 2015 by the University Press of Colorado

Published by Utah State University Press
An imprint of University Press of Colorado
5589 Arapahoe Avenue, Suite 206C
Boulder, Colorado 80303

 The University Press of Colorado is a proud member of
The Association of American University Presses.

The University Press of Colorado is a cooperative publishing enterprise supported, in part, by Adams State University, Colorado State University, Fort Lewis College, Metropolitan State University of Denver, Regis University, University of Colorado, University of Northern Colorado, Utah State University, and Western State Colorado University.

The paper used in this publication meets the minimum requirements of the American National Standard for Information Sciences—Permanence of Paper for Printed Library Materials. ANSI Z39.48–1992

ISBN: 978-0-87421-963-0 (paper)
ISBN: 978-0-87421-964-7 (ebook)

Library of Congress Cataloging-in-Publication Data
Rafoth, Bennett A.
  Multilingual writers and writing centers : Ben Rafoth.
    pages cm
  Includes bibliographical references and index.
  ISBN 978-0-87421-963-0 (pbk.) — ISBN 978-0-87421-964-7 (ebook)
1. Writing centers. 2. English language—Study and teaching—Foreign speakers. 3. Tutors and tutoring—Training of. I. Title.
  PE1404.R346 2014
  808'.042071—dc23
                            2014001150

Cover image © T30 Gallery / Shutterstock

CONTENTS

ACKNOWLEDGMENTS

I am grateful to many people for the ideas, support, encouragement, and feedback they offered as I worked on this book.

Many thanks to the tutors and writers who spoke or wrote to me about their work: Penelope Meyers, Christopher Minaya, Jose Luis Reyes Medina, Daniel Tehrani, and Kenisha Thomas at Bronx Community College; Valerie Makowiecki and Seungku Park at Indiana University of Pennsylvania; Westley Garcia at Northwestern College; Joanna DeCosse, Mehdi Rahimian, and Paulina Isabel Rogriguez at the University of Manitoba; Amanda Amionne, Brittany Bacallao, Christine Busser, Amanda Choi, Antoine Dahdah Sayegh, Alessia De Franco, Yohn Diaz, Shawnny Eugene, Natascha Faroh, Edgar Flores, Ariana Fonseca, Patrick Gourdet, Amione Jean, Crystal Mitchell, Rygo Morales, Joseph Nguyen, Dat Nguyen, Daniela Ortiz, Natalia Parra-Barrero, Hung (Harry) D. Pham, Denise Pichardo, Natalia Pinzon, Francesca Salomon, Sara Stanley, Daniel Thuman, and Alexandra Tuduce at Nova Southeastern University; Adeem Aa, Muneera Abdulmohsin AlAmer, Abeer Aloshan, and Dana Alsuhaim at Princess Nora Bint Abdulrahman University; Lisa Chason, Lee Jin Choi, Esther Dettmar, Yu-kyung Kang, John O'Connor, and Vanessa Rouillon at the University of Illinois Urbana-Champaign; and to the few who preferred to remain anonymous, thanks to you as well.

I offer special thanks to those who hosted, responded to, or inspired me at various points along the way: Khalid Abalhassan, Kathy Block, Shanti Bruce, Pisarn (Bee) Chamcharatsri, Leigh Ann Dunning, Kevin Dvorak, Libbie Morley, Andrea Olinger, Jan Robertson, Carol Severino, Taylor Snyder, and Tom Truesdell. I am especially grateful to Barbara Toth for sharing her thoughtful comments at critical moments, and to Jennifer Ritter for allowing me to use a transcribed session from her doctoral dissertation.

I also thank Yaw Asamoah, Timothy Moerland, Gian Pagnucci, and Tina Perdue for supporting my sabbatical to conduct

research and write this book. Many thanks to the superb editorial team at Utah State University Press—Michael Spooner,
Laura Furney, Kami Day, and Kelly Neumann. And finally, my
thanks to Mary Ann, Henry, and Paige for their support and
encouragement.

MULTILINGUAL WRITERS AND WRITING CENTERS

INTRODUCTION

How many layers of meaning must be peeled back to understand a word in context? Several? Several dozen? Lawyers, translators, teachers, and tutors are in business because language is a layer-cake of meanings. Whether the words are hard-to-translate ones like *dude* (American English) or *cafune* (Brazilian Portuguese), or deceptively simple ones like *boy, girl,* or *whatever,* words are only the beginning of the great chain of meaning. Arranged in columns and rows in a dictionary or thesaurus, words appear to contain only our thoughts, when in truth they do much more. Words also create a sense of belonging, exclusion, marginalization, and indifference. It is one thing to know grammar and vocabulary but quite another to know how to use language in specific, local contexts where one feels welcome and accepted. For this reason, even advanced learners of a second (or third, or more) language take the time to learn and practice nuanced meanings in that language and seek out informants—such as writing center tutors—to attain the linguistic, pragmatic, and sociocultural knowledge native speakers take for granted. Writing center tutors can be very helpful in this regard, but they must also strive to understand the various systems of linguistic knowledge that play out in the writing center. Such understanding calls for a new outlook among tutors and the directors who educate them.

This is a book written for writing center directors and tutors who take seriously the preparations needed to work with international multilingual students in the United States, or in any context where English is the dominant language. The book focuses on the changing face of writing centers and the implications of these changes on one-to-one interactions of tutoring. It explores this question: how can directors and tutors better

DOI: 10.7330/9780874219647.c000

prepare for the growing number of one-to-one conferences with multilingual writers who will come to their writing centers in the future?

Opportunities for tutors and directors to focus on one-to-one interactions in tutoring do not occur often enough. Such opportunities tend to emerge in discussions about other issues, such as why a tutor feels unable to get through to a writer, how a session got derailed, when to invoke a particular policy, or why a client gave a session a low evaluation. Sometimes they arise when trying to analyze a riveting exchange that happened in the span of a few seconds. When directors do get the chance to discuss their tutors' one-to-one interactions with writers, it is important for everyone to consider what is at stake for writers, what tutors are trying to help writers accomplish, and what tutors themselves stand to gain from these interactions.

This book draws upon three main sources of ideas: (1) over two decades of experience as a writing teacher and writing center director, (2) dozens of interviews I conducted with tutors, students, instructors, and directors at seven institutions in and outside the United States, and (3) published literature in the fields of writing centers, second language acquisition, second language writing, composition, and related areas. Most of my teaching experience has been at the graduate level in the composition and TESOL (teachers of English to speakers of other languages) program at Indiana University of Pennsylvania (IUP), which has attracted multilingual students and faculty from around the world for nearly four decades. It has taught me much about the intricate relationships students have with English, both here and in their home countries. These students have also been a source of talent for my writing center staff. While not as diverse as the graduate population, the peer tutors in the IUP Writing Center help reveal what motivates smart and ambitious learners. In this way, tutors are a lot like the international students who visit the writing center. They are impatient for success yet highly flexible when considering the terms on which success is offered.

Over the course of about nine months I communicated in person and via Skype and e-mail with eight directors and forty-one tutors. Two of these interviews were conducted with my own tutors. Except where noted, actual names are used with permission. I asked the tutors—most of whom were recommended to me by their directors—to tell me about the languages they speak and had studied and the significance of these languages to them personally. I asked them where they had lived and studied and to share any language teaching and learning events that made a difference for them personally and professionally. I also asked them what they had learned from their experiences as tutors, writers, and directors that I could share with others. I asked some of the same questions of the directors, including questions about the challenges and successes they faced in preparing tutors to work with multilingual writers. The questions became prompts for wide-ranging discussions.

I do not claim to pursue a formal research design, representative sample, or methodical analysis of the interviews, which I listened to multiple times and transcribed selectively, particularly when individuals addressed a theme or key point I wanted to explore in the book, or when they raised a new idea or perspective I felt belonged in it. The book offers neither a comprehensive plan nor a method for tutor education. Instead, it offers an informed invitation for writing center directors and their tutors, especially advanced tutors, to make greater use of theory and research from the field of second-language acquisition, particularly as it relates to one-to-one interaction, academic discourse, and providing corrective feedback. This theory and research expands the number and types of tools tutors can use to help writers. It gives insights into the effectiveness of practices and suggests ways to test this effectiveness. It can also, and perhaps ultimately, aid tutors in helping multilingual students become better writers.

AIM OF THIS BOOK

In most US writing centers, the assistance available for multilingual writers is not much different than it is for native speakers of English. Well intentioned and aware, writing center directors recognize multilingual writers need more assistance than most schools provide. Twenty years ago, however, Muriel Harris and Tony Silva (1993) called into question the quantity *and* the quality of this assistance: "Tutors, who bring to their work a background of experience and knowledge in interacting effectively with native speakers of English, are not adequately equipped to deal with some additional concerns of nonnative speakers of English—the unfamiliar grammatical errors, the sometimes bewilderingly different rhetorical patterns and conventions of other languages, and the expectations that accompany ESL writers when they come to the writing center" (526). The implication that tutors are better prepared to assist the native English-speaking students—who are most like them—has not been lost on the multilingual writers on today's campuses.

Harris and Silva suggest that tutors could "make minor accommodations in their tutoring style when working with ESL writers . . . who are used to hearing directive statements from teachers" (Harris and Silva 1993, 533) by asking fewer questions and making more open-ended requests—in other words, fewer *whys* and *hows* and more *please explains*. They write:

> Tutors who work with ESL students may have to be "tellers" to some extent because they will probably need to provide cultural, rhetorical, and/or linguistic information which native speakers intuitively possess and which ESL students do not have, but need to have to complete their writing assignments effectively. That is, regardless of their level of skill in collaboration or interpersonal interaction, tutors will not be able to elicit knowledge from ESL students if the students don't have that knowledge in the first place. (Harris and Silva 1993, 533)

If we can say ESL students are unable to draw upon knowledge they don't have in the first place, then the same must be said of tutors themselves. And while skills needed for collaboration and interaction are a component of all teachers' knowledge, these skills alone cannot make up for whatever tutors lack in conceptual knowledge. Tutors must be able to convey to writers, in one way or another, new information. To put it another way, when tutors are tellers, what is it that they tell? Do tutors know, and are they prepared to explain the linguistic, rhetorical, and cultural information we want them to be able to draw upon?

Questions about tutors' qualifications have been raised from time to time in the literature of writing centers. Shamoon and Burns's (1995) article "A Critique of Pure Tutoring" challenges directors to step back from the self-imposed requirement for nondirective tutoring and consider approaches that respond more favorably to students' needs for development of their cognitive skills. Paul Kei Matsuda (2012) also asks writing center administrators to examine their assumptions, including the reliance on peer tutors instead of professional teachers with expertise in second-language instruction. He writes, "Peer tutors, who are by definition sympathetic readers but not experts in the teaching of writing or language, may not be able to meet the needs of clients who have an advanced knowledge of the subject and discipline-specific genres yet are struggling to express their ideas in the second language" (48). While the statement that tutors are merely sympathetic readers and not experts ignores the critical reading and skills that many tutors possess, Matsuda's argument suggests that peer tutors sometimes identify too closely with those they are supposed to help and remain too far removed from the knowledge and skills needed to be helpful. Matsuda points to specific tutor practices, such as focusing on global issues (content, organization, and ideas) over and above local matters (grammar, style, and mechanics). Experienced writers know that global and local issues operate on many levels at once, and good writers learn to traverse these levels with aplomb.

Preparing tutors to help writers navigate these levels is the responsibility of all directors. Most are fortunate enough to work with tutors who rank among the best and brightest students on campus, and it is in everyone's best interest to move beyond the simplistic dichotomy—identified a decade and a half ago by Susan Blau, John Hall, Sarah and Sparks (2002)—between global and local errors. In addition, tutors must be prepared to take full advantage, both for their clients and themselves, of the learning opportunities unique to the one-to-one conference. They must be familiar with academic discourse and its variations by purpose and discipline; with errors and how to explain them; and with the struggles and rewards—both their own and others'—of learning and learning about languages.

This book is a call to directors to ask more of their tutors and themselves. It seeks to answer some of the questions currently plaguing writing centers across the United States: What can directors learn about concepts and practices in the field of second-language acquisition (SLA)? How can they borrow from SLA to help tutors respond to the needs of multilingual writers? How can they lead tutors toward greater curiosity about multilingual writers and their writing? These questions are a start, but they presume we have been thinking about the answer to another question: how might tutoring change as our student populations change? One approach is to consider the many demands advanced literacy makes on all students, even graduate students with advanced levels of English proficiency, and then find ways to adapt to a changing environment.

WHICH PHONE IS IT?

Esther Dettmar is a graduate consultant in the Writers Workshop on the campus of the University of Illinois Urbana-Campaign. The morning's first appointment was with Mei (not her name), a Chinese L1 with a master's degree from Arizona State University. She was working on revising the draft of an abstract for a longer paper she was writing. Mei took several minutes to describe her project for her tutor: she was writing about three similar products and wanted to make sure her reader could follow which was which as she described them. Esther and Mei decided that Mei would read the paper aloud because it was about a page and a half in length, and Mei seemed ready to do so. After she had read her paper aloud, she paused to wait for feedback from her tutor.

On the surface, this seemed to be a fairly straightforward writing task and one that almost any tutor could manage. Mei was articulate, the paper was short, the problem was specific, and the goal seemed clear: make sure three different products are clearly identified for readers. In the space of a few minutes, however, the challenges Mei faced became clear. One was linguistic: English uses a complex system of lexical links to refer to things in a text that have already been mentioned (*this, they, one*) and things that will be mentioned later (*next, a/an*). Words like *this/that, these/those,* and others interact in subtle ways to direct the reader's attention to persons, places, ideas, or objects the writer wants to bring into focus. Even advanced learners can have a hard time using lexical links to make clear, in writing, their intention to refer to one thing and not another—*this one* not *that one,* or *any one* and not *one in particular.* Cohesion—in the specialized sense used in linguistics to denote a complex system of lexical and grammatical links writers and readers use to make sense of a text—has been studied extensively (Halliday and Hasan 1976) and presents a high hurdle for language learners.

It is not hard to imagine how difficult cohesion becomes when the writer is a nonnative English speaker (NNES) and she is writing about multiple, similar objects. In Mei's case, they were three mobile phones. Two of them were fully designed and developed Nokia smart phones—one of these two was marketed to consumers by the company and the other was not—and the third was an Apple smart phone. In addition, each phone was also an example of a phenomenon in a mathematical model Mei was using as part of her larger analysis of consumer-marketing strategies. Therefore, the physical phones as well as the "phone phenomena" had to be kept distinct from one another (except when they were grouped) as the writer introduced the topic, focused it, described the products and the theoretical model, and explained the phones' relationships to the model and its components. An additional challenge Mei faced, then, was that her ideas were complex and highly analytical. They required a facility with verbal expression that was advanced by any measure.

Mei asked the consultant, "When I say 'first example' and 'second example' and so on, is it clear that Nokia has two phones and Apple has one?"

Sensing that this question was one of those that tugs at the yarn that unravels the shawl, Esther paused for a moment.

Both Esther and Mei understood that keeping the phones distinct in the reader's mind was a key focus for the session. Esther projected a measured confidence that they would reach this goal, but she could see that Mei's proficiency with English was good but not quite good enough to manage the multiple references on her own. Besides, writing an abstract can be tricky. In the longer paper she was writing, Mei could use repetition and redundancy to keep the reader on track with the various mobile phones. An abstract, however, demands conciseness. Had Mei taken her paper to a friend, it is unlikely she would have received the painstakingly close attention to reference words and conciseness that Esther provided; she might have gotten instead a few trivial corrections on her grammar. When Mei came to the writing center, she found there a consultant who knew how to navigate her way through complicated texts and how to help others do likewise. In the simple terms of writing centers, Mei had a draft and needed feedback. In the more precise terms of applied linguistics, what Mei put on the table was *output*; what she needed from her tutor was *comprehensible input* along with *negotiated interaction* and *recasting*. In the vernacular of writing centers, Mei had a draft and needed feedback.

After the pause, Mei and Esther talked more about what Mei was trying to say and the difficulty of keeping the three phones and their corresponding phone phenomena separate and distinct. They jumped to one of the places where confusion arose and worked on it. Before going on, Esther raised her head, took a breath, and said, "Let's go back to the top and read line by line, and when I don't understand which product you are referring to, we'll stop and work on it, okay?" Mei nodded.

As agreed, they started in. For the first few places where they stopped, Esther either explained her confusion or Mei preempted discussion with an explanation, sometimes lasting minutes. Esther listened intently while keeping an eye on keywords in the text and ignoring others that did not interfere with comprehension. They went back and forth until there was clarity, as Mei typed away on her keyboard. Seeing that this approach was working, Esther formalized the process: "Again, I'm going to say now in my own words what I think you just said, and that way I'll know, myself, if I understand what you're saying." Mei then either nodded agreement to Esther's understanding or corrected or clarified it until Esther understood and could state her understanding clearly. Then Mei typed, usually an abbreviated form or phrase to help her remember when she went back later and made the changes on her own. They were deep into the minutiae of phones and phone phenomena.

Usually, after running her fingers through her hair to help her concentrate, Esther verbalized her own attempts to understand Mei's text: "So Nokia's first phone is what you mean here when you say 'this phone' or later over here when you say 'the phone.' Is that right?" or she would say, "And 'this' refers to the previous attempt, I think?" If Mei agreed with Esther, she typed in the change, using Esther's words or her own. Esther didn't let the conference become sidetracked with other matters. When a resolution seemed to be close at hand, Esther would say, "Let's move on."

Several things stand out in this thoughtful and productive tutoring session. First, Mei began learning English in school in China from an early age, earned a college degree in China, and is now an advanced international student with five years in the United States. She is working on her doctorate in business administration. Mei speaks English fluently, but says she comes to the Writers Workshop for help with her academic English. Had Mei been writing in her native Chinese and without the strict demands that conciseness puts on every word, the reference problem would still have been tricky, but it is something she could have managed on her own. For a nonnative speaker, however, navigating English's reference system can feel like getting lost in an M. C. Escher drawing, full of twists, turns, and never-ending loops. Possessing advanced literacy in both her native language and English means that some aspects of English will still be difficult for her. Even with repeated exposure and effort, proficiency with these aspects may never be fully acquired, and tutors are often the writer's only hope of finding the words and phrases that make success in writing possible.

Second, the session unfolds as an example of tutoring and learning in the *zone of proximal development*, or the idea that people learn new things by building upon what they already know with help from a more capable partner. To facilitate this learning, teachers and tutors assume that something people can learn to do with assistance or cooperatively with others, they can then eventually do on their own. In this case, the consultant used the teaching and learning technique of *scaffolding* to shape the language Mei needed. With a native English speaker (NES) scaffolding is still essential, but Esther would have relied more heavily on the client's intuitions about words "sounding right." Mei's English was very good, but she did not have the same intuitions as a native speaker, and the standard for accuracy in her writing was very high. Sometimes the consultant filled in thoughts or words to confirm her meaning or she probed Mei's words for clarity, and sometimes she moved the session along to the next line or problem, each time helping Mei to do as much of the work as she could. They frequently tested the link between words and meaning by reading, listening, speaking, and writing. What is not so apparent are the precise ways in which the consultant worked cooperatively with Mei by using various pragmatic devices to question, suggest, doubt, affirm, and so on. Like any good tutor, Esther brought curiosity, energy, and attentiveness to the conference, but these were combined with both her tacit and explicit knowledge of cohesive ties, how texts work to create meaning, and how to interact with Mei through a modified conversation. Mei is bright and motivated, and writers like her need tutors who are able to work at an advanced level. By the end of the session, Mei felt a clear sense of accomplishment. "She's really good," Mei said appreciatively.

A third thing that stands out in this session is the way in which the consultant employs the technique of *recasting*. Upon hearing and reading a phrase in Mei's text that was unclear, Esther stopped and either inquired further of Mei or recast what she had heard in a way that suggested rewording and made the referent clearer. Recasting can be a valuable technique when writers are unable to make a correction on their own because they do not recognize the error. For example, in other contexts, a tutor might recast when a student writes "Apple market's share falls one percent." The tutor would then read it aloud as "Apple's market share falls one percent?" by inserting and stressing the correct form, repeating *apple* to indicate a problem, and raising the intonation to ask for confirmation—"Is this what you intended to say, and do you understand and accept the change?" Recasting is achieved by pairing implicit negative feedback (interrupting) with implicit positive feedback (providing the correct form) (Byrd, 2005). Esther's recast frames her feedback as a check on her own understanding while at the same time giving feedback to the writer that something is wrong and suggesting an alternative. Recasting is one of many techniques, and tutors should use it judiciously, but when used appropriately it can be the only way to make progress in a tutoring session.

A great variety of papers make their way to the writing center, and many are at least as complex as Mei's and are often longer. Tutors as thoughtful and adept as Esther are treasures. But from micro to macro levels, the conference between Esther and Mei hints at the challenges we face when we think and talk about one-to-one tutoring with multilingual writers. For example, does Esther need to be able to explain the cohesive structure of a text in order to help Mei use clear references, or is it enough that Esther is familiar with how an abstract is supposed to sound? Does Mei rely too much on Esther when Esther speaks and Mei types, or is this the best way for Mei to learn new forms of the language and produce writing acceptable to her professor? Would it have helped Esther to know something about Chinese, Mei's L1, or is it better to conduct the conference entirely in English?

HIGH EXPECTATIONS

We expect tutors to figure out what writers are able to learn on their own and what requires help, as well as what kind of help is needed and where to begin. Tutors are supposed to be able to confirm that writers are making progress and know what to do when they haven't. We expect tutors to describe papers, structures, and sessions and to consult with us about problems as they arise. At other levels, the sociocultural and interpersonal, we want tutors to bring to all sessions a genuine interest in and curiosity about the writers and their writing: Who are they and where do they come from? What do they want to write about? How can I learn something about their first languages and schooling to better understand the interferences that may be occurring? These questions imply an intricate understanding of the challenges NNES students face, particularly when their tutors lack the understanding and the tools needed to develop it.

A number of writing center scholars such as Frankie Condon (2012), Harry Denny (2010), Nancy Grimm (1999), Greenfield and Rowan (2011), Michelle Cox et al. (2011), and others have recognized that raising tutors' awareness, especially awareness of writers' identities, is a key first step for working with diverse populations of students. Grimm, for example, observes that tutors cannot be expected, initially, to have the vocabulary, self-awareness, or confidence to engage with writers to the degree we would like. For Grimm, directors play an important role in giving tutors the opportunity to see themselves, as well as their clients, "as raced, classed, gendered, and multiply situated" selves because mainstream, white, Western (mostly) tutors need help in recognizing that such notions as responsible tutor, good student, and good writing cannot be taken as natural or normal; these concepts are institutionally defined and constructed. To look beyond them, tutors must be encouraged by directors and other educators to imagine their own identities, and others', differently.

> By developing and demonstrating awareness of the formation and reformation of their identity, writing center tutors, no matter how awkwardly they do this, can encourage the creation of transitional space where they can play with and challenge cultural expectations, reimagining social futures. (Grimm 1999, 76)

Writing centers serve students from many backgrounds, disciplines, academic levels, and abilities. In many cases, multilingual writers have significantly more grammatical knowledge of English, worldly experience, and advanced literacy in their native language than their native English-speaking tutors do. As tutors achieve the kind of greater sociocultural awareness that Grimm and others call for, how do we want them to work with these writers in the writing conference? For example, there can be no doubt we want tutors who can recognize diverse student populations and the consequences that privilege and marginalization can have for students' writing. We want tutors who understand and can identify with culturally and linguistically diverse populations of writers. But we also want tutors who possess the kind of strategic knowledge for helping second-language writers that the field of SLA has made us aware of. Do we know what this strategic knowledge is and have we tried to teach it to our tutors? Have we taught them, for example, how to gain a sense of what writers know and can accomplish on their own versus only with help? Do directors know enough about the structures of English to be able to recognize and discuss forms and functions at the level of phrases, clauses, and larger pieces of discourse? And do tutors know who they can turn to as a source for acquiring the knowledge and skills they are expected to possess but don't yet have?

Questions like these go to the heart of scholarly, professional, and personal responsibilities. In this book, I aim to provoke directors and tutors to reflect on these questions, share them with one another, and use examples from the real-life tutoring sessions provided as a guide in their own attempts at improving writing center curricula. In each chapter, I pick out a different aspect—and consequently a different challenge—of a tutoring session that might be improved. In the first chapter, I offer snapshots of writing centers in various places around the world in order to show their growing diversity. I introduce multilingual writers who bring high expectations to the writing center for what they will be able to accomplish in the relatively brief time of a writing conference. Their high expectations stem from their intimate knowledge of the tremendous challenge posed by learning advanced literacy in English, their second (or third, or more) language, and the challenges posed by English vocabulary, syntax, collocations, and cultural references. At the same time, tutors' knowledge and skills to help them meet these challenges are often less than optimal.

The second chapter shows how tutorial conversations can be made more instructive by negotiating the interaction and taking advantage of opportunities created by miscommunication. I discuss the choices tutors must make when deciding whether to simply tell the student the correct answer or help them get there on their own. I bring up the tendency students have to request native English-speaking tutors and the perceived superiority that represents. I also discuss the importance of listening in tutor-student interaction and how listening relates to the ways NNES students learn English. The process of learning a first language can be different from learning a second, and the way in which one learns a new language plays an important role in the writing center. I consider the effect of miscommunication on language learning and relay the importance of tutors' familiarity with concepts of language acquisition in order to understand what the student may be going through. Knowing more about language learning is a key step for developing more effective tutorial interactions.

Chapter 3 delves more specifically into academic writing and its many nuances. The skills required to be verbally proficient in general only increase as students move into academia, and sometimes NNES students do not have the lexicon required to handle the thousands of different words in an academic text. I discuss the challenges multilingual students face in meeting the demands instructors make on their academic writing and whether the expectations are appropriate for these students. Too often, work on writing is sidetracked by students' struggles to meet the formatting requirements teachers place on their assignments. Consequently, students rely on tools, such as translators, to help them expand their vocabularies and write papers their teachers won't rip to shreds. Tutors must understand the increased challenges multilingual students have when writing an academic paper and they must be able to help their students scale the language barrier and be successful writers.

In chapter 4, I take up the idea of corrective feedback, specifically the differences between helpful feedback and feedback that hinders successful writing. While sometimes correcting every error is necessary and useful, in certain situations it is more helpful to focus on serious transgressions while leaving trivial ones for students to discover on their own. I discuss the ways in which tutors can bring attention to these errors and how that attention can impact how much or how little the information is retained for further use. Tutors must encourage students to notice their own mistakes and then discuss them in a way that leads the students to know how to fix them.

I conclude by discussing the ways we as educators, directors, and mentors can help prepare our tutors—and ourselves—to work with multilingual students in the writing center. Chapter 5 introduces some of the research on what tutors should know in order to best serve their students. It considers the ongoing debate on how involved tutors should be in their students' writing and whether university policies against helping them at the sentence level prevent multilingual writers from learning the idiosyncrasies of English and what their native teachers expect from them. I close by emphasizing the importance of working with the faculty and other members of the university to help students succeed in the best way possible. By helping educators to understand the issues facing multilingual writers today, we can overcome language barriers and usher students into the globalized world prepared for whatever it may bring.

CONCLUSION

Some of the criticisms made of writing center tutors—such as that they lack sufficient expertise in second-language writing—can and have been made of instructors who teach second-language students in their writing courses. The criticisms are often misplaced. Admission policies, placement mechanisms, and resources all factor in to what students need and how well we can respond to these needs. But sometimes the criticisms are accurate and make a larger point. United States colleges and universities operate in a culture that idealizes Standard American English; tutors and the faculty members who teach them are usually English focused and lack preparation for teaching second-language writers and writing. As Paul Matsuda (2006) has observed, "Writing programs in U.S. higher education—as well as the intellectual field of composition studies, which has grown out of that particular historical and institutional context—have been based on the assumption of English monolingualism as the norm" (637).

The culture of *monolingualism* grows among racial and cultural stereotypes on the hard clay of ignorance and isolation. Over decades, the assumptions of English monolingualism were convenient for academic leaders who devoted few curricular resources to multilingual learners, including courses in language, culture, linguistics, and rhetoric taught by specialists. Writing center directors and other leaders have made progress in addressing some of the problems associated with monolingualism and have welcomed other languages and cultures to the writing center (Babcock and Thonus 2012; Condon 2012; CCCC 2009; Denny 2010; Greenfield and Rowan 2011). Yet there is still a long way to go. The next steps will require directors to open the doors wider, inform and advocate, and develop a praxis of tutor education that draws knowledge from the fields of second-language writing and applied linguistics.

At stake in these discussions are the hopes of writers like Rico, who was born in Venezuela and came to the United States when he was fifteen. His yearning for education is the sort that makes teachers and tutors want to connect with him. He smiled broadly when he told me, "The best way [for an L2 writer] to get help is to write whatever they want and then have the tutor go over it and explain every mistake. Grammar is the most important thing. You need to know why that word goes there or why that sentence is right. That's what we need." Rico says "grammar" and "mistake," but if pressed he might mean any number of things, like rhetorical choices, transitions, cohesive ties, clarifying devices, colloquialisms, collocations, and other features that only writing teachers know the names for. What comes through loud and clear as he talks, though, is the desire for more instruction, more "going over," and more explaining.

It would be easy enough to dismiss such requests as admirable but unrealistic: what writing center has the resources to satisfy such a hunger for learning? Yet in Rico's recorded interview, one hears the stress he places on "go over it" and "explain," and it seems clear that he is not so much asking for unlimited tutoring as telling how hard he himself is prepared to work at learning English. A. Suresh Canagarajah (2006b) notes that diversity demands more, not less, from minority students: "They have to not only master the dominant varieties of English, but also know how to bring in their preferred varieties in rhetorically strategic ways" (598). Gaining these rhetorical strategies requires tutors who can look at writing such as Rico's, analyze its strengths and weaknesses, and help the writer to zero in on the next steps they need to take, not merely affirming their efforts or offering boilerplate advice.

Whether or not tutoring sessions such as this are typical or even possible is for readers to judge, but in the professional conversation and scholarly research of writing centers, there is a dearth of discussion about them. To respond to writers like Rico, tutors must bring a fair amount of knowledge and experience to the table, and much of this knowledge is rarely taught or available to tutors. Directors are nonetheless an important source of this knowledge, or at least they are the first point of contact for tutors. Both directors and tutors have a responsibility to expand the knowledge base for themselves and others because writing centers are part of the hope and inspiration that public higher education holds out to everyone. I hope members of the writing center community will see in this book an optimism about the future of writing centers as well as a call to invigorate the preparation of tutors and directors for the multilingual futures that await us all.

1

THE CHANGING FACES OF WRITING CENTERS

From the time they were laboratories in the first half of the last century until today, one hundred years later, writing centers have evolved with higher education generally and the teaching of writing in particular. Writing centers have been around a long time and have made a difference in the lives of many students. Today, the face of writing centers is changing along with the worldwide expansion of educational opportunities. The foundation of writing center pedagogy—one-to-one instruction—is still a critical asset in the writing curriculum, but it is also labor—and intellectually—intensive, meaning that there are not enough well-qualified tutors to meet students' needs. Growing numbers of students from around the world turn to writing centers to learn to write in their native languages and in English, and at advanced levels. They seek degrees that will usher them and their families into the modern economy and secure their futures with good education and rewarding careers. Writing program administrators seek the same thing for themselves, in fact. Chris Thaiss et al. (2012) observe that "the drive to become literate and, therefore, to teach literacy, usually in advanced forms, is sparked in almost every case by student and staff desires for academic recognition in the international research community or by desire for career success in the global economy" (9). People everywhere want many of the same things.

Education and jobs are intertwined with a host of other motivations. Among the students I interviewed, the desire to be good citizens, partners, and family members as well as to find

DOI: 10.7330/9780874219647.c001

happiness all had personal roots tied to education and careers. These are the life goals for millions of people abroad and in the United States who pursue dreams at great cost to themselves and their loved ones. In rural China, for instance, according to an article in the *New York Times* (Bradsher, Feb. 17, 2013), families make sacrifices to sponsor college attendance for one or more of their members on incomes that average around $5,000 a year. The report calculates the annual cost of higher education at a Chinese university for a rural family to be between six and fifteen months' labor. For a Chinese family to send a member to college in the United States can cost not only a lifetime's worth of savings but much of their income while the child is growing up—for boarding schools, special tutors, and language classes. Moreover, proficiency in English is not just a requirement for getting into schools in the United States, the United Kingdom, Australia, Ireland, and other popular destinations—it is also needed for admission to most good Chinese universities. Given how intent so many students are on learning advanced English, are today's writing centers ready for them?

MORE WRITING, MORE WRITING CENTERS

Families around the globe are helping to escalate college enrollments that are changing the face of higher education worldwide. In the growth economies of Asia, Brazil, India, and China, new university campuses are springing up in record time and established ones can barely expand fast enough to meet demand. College enrollments worldwide are expected to grow by twenty-one million students by 2020 according to a study conducted for the British Council (Sharma, *University World News*, March 13, 2012). This represents a huge rise in overall numbers and an average growth rate of 1.4 percent per year. China, India, and the United States will continue to see increases, while the fastest growth is expected to occur in Brazil, Indonesia, Turkey, and Nigeria. The study projects that the largest higher education systems will likely be China with thirty-seven million students, India with twenty-eight million, the United States with twenty million, and Brazil with nine million. Elsewhere, Mexico has opened seventy-five new colleges and universities since 2006 (Lloyd 2010). In Saudi Arabia, thirty-five new colleges and universities have opened since 2000. India plans to double the number of students enrolled in higher education and open about 200 new universities in the next five years (Chauhan, *Hindustan Times*, April 25, 2012).

For US higher education, this rise in student numbers means continued growth in the population of international students as increasing prosperity overseas creates opportunities for travel, immigration, study abroad, and graduate education, with the United States being a preferred destination. For writing centers, this growth means more multilingual and multicompetent writers (Cook 1999) for whom English is but one resource in their communicative repertoire. A tutor's knowledge of another language is valuable not only for the cultural insights it gives them but also for the shared experience of language learning and figuring out how to overcome communication obstacles. Learning a new language builds pedagogical skills most monolingual writers take for granted. People who live and work among multiple languages acquire skills for gauging when and how to move between languages, and they learn a greater variety of the expectations people have for different kinds of conversational interaction. According to Canagarajah (2006a), multilingual students no longer see themselves as located within one language or another but as shuttling between languages to achieve their diverse goals for communication.

For today's NNES students, these goals will continue to include control over the academic discourses of English. To achieve this control, though, they will use all the resources available to them, including tutors, teachers, peers, family members, online translators, textual borrowing, and downloadable apps. Writing centers will still be a tool for gaining advanced literacy and a place where tutors help students, in one-to-one conferences, to express their thoughts. But instead of language proficiency, says Canagarajah (2009), in the future "the versatility with which we can do things with words" (20) will matter most.

And while English may remain dominant, the advantage that multicompetent, multilingual users have over monolinguals will only increase.

This advantage is apparent in multilingual tutoring sessions. Miguel, a tutor at Bronx Community College who is bilingual in Spanish and English, described for me a difficult session he had not long ago that started out in English. The writer was a female history major. "She pushed me to answer all her questions and didn't want to think things through," he said. "She became very agitated." So, Miguel switched to Spanish and they continued to talk for a while. "She was very anxious when we talked in English," he said, "but in Spanish, she calmed down. Spanish created comfort for her." I asked him how he knew when to switch back to English, and he said, "When the student reads the assignment and we see concepts—these have to be understood. That, we do in English." He added, "Being sympathetic to the language of students helps. It says you recognize, 'I am dealing with two languages here. It's real. It's hard.'"

In the United States today, most enrollment increases in higher education come not from domestic but from international students, and it is easy to see why they and other multilingual students like Miguel are becoming writing center tutors. According to a report in the *Chronicle of Higher Education* (McMurtrie 2012), the number of international students grew faster in 2011 than it did in the previous two years. Saudi students have enrolled at record levels, up by 50 percent in recent years and now numbering well over forty thousand, due in part to scholarship support by the government. Growth was especially strong in programs offering the bachelor's degree and those offering English-language instruction. According to figures generated by NAFSA: Association of International Educators, international students and their dependents contributed $21.8 billion to the American economy in tuition and living expenses. These numbers are likely to rise as more international students are welcomed into the country. In 2012, for example, President Obama promised an increase in the number of student visas from Latin America and the

Caribbean from sixty-four thousand to one hundred thousand. Issuing visas is only the first step toward an education, however. According to an administrator for international programs at the University of Kansas, "As they increase international enrollments, [colleges] need to bolster the services surrounding them, from English-language classes to academic advising to extracurricular activities. We can't be bringing students here to fail" (McMurtrie 2012).

Along with the growth of higher education around the world and in the United States have come organizations for networking and professional development: the European Association for the Teaching of Academic Writing (EATAW), the International Society for the Advancement of Writing Research, the International Research Foundation for English Language Education (TIRF), the International WAC/WID Mapping Project, and the newest affiliates of the International Writing Centers Association—the European Writing Centers Association (EWCA) and the Middle East-North Africa Writing Centers Alliance (MENAWCA). In addition, there are untold numbers of local and regional affiliations of writing centers and writing programs. These organizations provide opportunities for directors' professional development and new ways for them to educate tutors to help students learn to write in English and their native languages. As more organizations join in helping improve writing center tutors' effectiveness and their clients' writing, more resources will be available to expand writing center values even further.

WRITING CENTER SNAPSHOTS HERE AND ABROAD

Thaiss et al. (2012) have provided a sense of the diversity of writing programs and writing centers around the world, as well as the ways those writing centers have organized literacy education in response to their cultures' pedagogical traditions and students' needs. The many programs and centers featured in their book explore structures outside their borders for teaching and learning. They show how these structures have arisen in response to the internationalizing of English-language teaching, especially for academic and professional purposes, and how the teaching of writing has been enhanced by the accessibility of Internet-based resources. Thaiss et al. (2012) offer at least four reasons that help explain the burgeoning interest these program have shown for exploring writing instruction: (1) the transnationality of education and the centrality of learning English, (2) the desire for advanced literacy, (3) the range of linguistic and cultural backgrounds among teachers and students, and (4) the influence of mass culture on the kinds of literacy education they seek (9).

One or more of these reasons now applies to almost every writing center, in the United States as well as overseas, because multilingualism has begun to define what it means to teach and learn in a writing center. To get a better feel for this diversity and the impact we can expect from it, we can look into the windows, so to speak, of a handful of writing centers around the world. Massey University spans three campuses in New Zealand. It has a greater percentage of Maori students than any other university on the island. About half of its thirty-four thousand students are enrolled in distance education. Political and economic dislocations from the mid-1980s to the mid-1990s focused attention on nontraditional groups, especially those who were older and less affluent. For the first time, they were able to take advantage of programs to prepare for second careers and learn new skills. Indigenous people benefitted as well. To serve students unable to travel to campus, the university's Online Writing and Learning Link was created to provide a library of resources (Emerson 2012).

In Istanbul, Turkey, Sabanci University has long supported efforts that promote international outreach. Its writing center has participated in various regional and international organizations, including NCTE and CCCC in the United States. "As we mix with others, we add to the international common core of knowledge, and we then bring back what we have observed and admired as differences, to be shared by others at home and implemented as much as the circumstances allow," says

Dilek Tokay, Sabanci's former writing center director. Tokay herself served as chair of the 2005 European Writing Centers Association conference, and in 2010, the IWCA honored her for her many contributions to the organization (Tokay 2012).

Located in one of the most densely populated areas in the United States, Bronx Community College in New York draws students from one of the most diverse communities in the nation. The Bronx is proud of its diversity and boasts that if you were to randomly select any two people in the Bronx, there is an 89 percent chance they would belong to different racial or ethnic groups. More than two decades ago, Puerto Ricans made up a quarter of the population. The number of Dominicans, Cubans, Jamaicans, Koreans, Vietnamese, Indians, Pakistanis, Greeks, and Russians has climbed dramatically since then. Albanians settled in the Belmont area, Cambodians in Fordham. Luxury apartments built in Riverdale in the 1950s became cooperatives. The Bronx has the world's largest concentration of buildings in the art deco style. Against this backdrop, the community college writing center is home to twenty-six tutors who speak Spanish, French, Arabic, Urdu, Hindi, Bangla, Farsi, Turkish, Ewe (Ghana), Twi (Ghana), Patwa (north India), and Chichewa (Malawi). A majority of the students they serve is Hispanic, but the linguistic bouquet among the students is as varied as it is for the tutors. The BCC center is also one of the busiest in the country, with over seven thousand one-to-one tutoring sessions per year.

In Riyadh, Saudi Arabia, three new writing centers have debuted, including the first writing center at an all-Muslim women's university. The Princess Nora Bint Abdulrahman University Writing Center is unique because it was started by a midwesterner from the United States, Dr. Barbara Toth, and it has grown from 150 to over one thousand tutoring sessions in its first two years of operation. Muneer AlAmer, one of the tutors, described it to me this way:

> It has three floors. The first floor has a library for those who want to borrow, and the second floor has computers for those who need to use the Internet and look up certain topics. Finally, the

third floor has a meeting room for consultants to discuss about the students they come in. Also, it is where we meet students and help them with their writings. Moreover, we have an access to the largest databases on Internet. It helps us a lot when we need some reliable resources about topics related to writing. Everyone works in the writing center is very cooperative and willing to help in any way.

On the other side of town is the campus of King Abdulaziz University, where irrigated flowers and palm trees line the roads in and out of a vast complex of buildings. The KAU writing centers are housed in two brand-new, identical buildings, one dedicated to Arabic and one to English, each with its own auditorium for workshops, speakers, and presentations. Tutors work with writers near the buildings' exterior glass walls, so they are visible from the sidewalks outside. Support for Arabic literacy is part of KAU's mission, and the writing centers are seen as having a key role. Faculty members at KAU and other Arabic universities rely on professional materials written in Arabic, and they seek to publish their research in English- and Arabic-language scholarly journals. It is significant that KAU decided to keep the Arabic and English writing centers separate. Had they been combined, one language or the other might have dominated, and they wanted to keep that from happening. Dr. Khalid Abalhassan, a linguist and a former IUP writing center intern, formed a task force to create a nationwide plan to establish writing centers in Saudi universities and secondary schools. Khalid explained the rationale to me: "Establishing writing centers in Saudi Arabia requires the presence of collaborative learning culture, respect for intellectual property, and a sense of ownership about one's writing and research." As an adviser to the vice minister for educational affairs in Saudi Arabia, Khalid believes that implementation of the plan will allow writing centers to influence how students learn, and are taught, in Saudi universities.

Eight time zones from KAU, in the small farming town of Orange City, Iowa, is Northwestern College, a private Christian liberal arts school. The state of Iowa is located in the middle of the United States, and Orange City, population 6,004, is located in the middle of Iowa. Calling it a rural farming town is considered high praise by most residents, many of whom settled here from Holland and refer to themselves as Dutch. To a visitor, the town might seem like one of the least diverse places in the country; about 93 percent of its residents are white. Hispanics/Latinos, Asians, and other races make up the rest. But census data are imperfect and don't reflect specific locales. Thinking that the writing center tutors would have a better feel for the diversity of the campus than an outsider could perceive in a two-day visit, I asked one of the tutors, Alanna (not her real name), to describe in writing the college's writing center when I visited. She gave me this third-person snapshot.

> Alanna walked into the center, tired after a long day. She is Puerto Rican with a brilliant smile. She sat next to a Nepali boy, Suraj, who was having difficulty with his marketing essay. He had his whole paper ready in his mind but didn't know how to start it. Alanna calmed him down and walked him through his essay. Later, Noriko, a Japanese freshman walked in looking a little worried. She saw me and walked over. I am Indian born and raised in Bahrain. She's one of my regulars and tonight, she had a huge task in hand—an essay on Place. We brainstormed ideas and worry slowly turned into hope. Noriko was going to do just fine on her essay. In the midst of the silence in the room, Wes, whose parents are from Mexico and El Salvador and grew up in California, giggled in the corner. It's a giggle that's unique to him. Everyone knows when Wes is around. He was working with Enid, a very Dutch sophomore from Orange City. I guess she had something really funny in her essay. We have different stories and heritages and we come together in a room and connect.

Another tutor, Westley Garcia, tried to explain Northwestern's diversity from a faith perspective.

> I am infinitely fascinated with the Christian ideological diversity displayed by tutors. Ian, for example, grew up in the Christian Reformed Church and lives out the understanding that God has predestined certain people for salvation. Diametrically opposed you find me, Westley, a Christian Universalist, who sees Jesus Christ's sacrifice as bridging the schism that prevents a relationship with God. Sienna, Hannah, and Sue Ann are three

liberal Christians who believe in the full inclusion of woman and LGBTQ members as the true expression of redemption. Noah and other tutors have a Christian faith that manifests in neither an evangelical or progressive persuasion, but one that is intimately personal and reserved. And then there's Cathleen, who grew up in a Muslim country but professes a Christian faith. Or Janice, who grew up in the US a Christian, but now professes a Muslim faith. A wide and diverse spectrum of faiths are expressed at Northwestern College. It is an environment that serves to encourage tutees in their wrestling of concepts, but also provides a rich environment for the exchange of ideas.

The Centre for Academic Writing at Coventry University in the United Kingdom and the Regional Writing Centre at the University of Limerick are two of the many examples of universities outside the United States that house their entire writing programs in their writing centers. Writing across the curriculum, writing in the disciplines, research, and publication resources are also found there. One of the interesting aspects of this model is the ability of these centers to create curriculum in the form of courses, workshops, videos, and other instructional materials that align with the pedagogical philosophy of the writing center.

In 2008, the European University Viadrina started a program of peer tutoring, the first in Germany. Four of these peer tutors went on to publish the first German book about writing tutoring and consulting, and several of the faculty who taught them have now started the Gesellschaft für Schreibdidaktik und Schreibforschung, an association for professionals and peer tutors dedicated to writing center work and writing consulting. Ten scholars, led by Katrin Girgensohn (Viadrina University) and Melanie Brinkschulte (Göttingen University), established the association and plan to offer a certificate for those who complete a basic module on writing center theory and practice that focuses on the specialization of different writing centers around the country, such as reading pedagogies, multilingualism, and writing across the curriculum. The association also plans to offer a master's degree in the theory and practice of writing and writing centers.

These are only a few of the changing faces of writing centers, changes driven by enrollment growth on their campuses and the desire for advanced literacy in virtually all disciplines. These snapshots offer a glimpse of writing centers as they operate today, and they give but a hint of the linguistic and cultural diversity headed to a writing center near you.

MULTILINGUAL VARIETY

Whether you gaze broadly at the span of changes brought about by multilingualism or look narrowly at the depth of these changes, familiar concepts like language, dialect, and standard strain to describe what is happening on college campuses in the United States, Canada, and elsewhere. When English and at least one other language are spoken in a writing center on a regular basis, what is the center's official language? If two students who cannot understand each other claim they speak different dialects but the same language, who's to argue about the definition of a dialect versus a language? When a writing assignment insists that students use Standard English, which Standard English would that be, exactly? Do we want tutors to help writers stick to the standard or to express their ideas clearly?

Linguists have never quite been able to define terms like *language, dialect,* or *standard* in a way that holds true for any of these terms. While the terms are still used as shorthand, most linguists prefer *linguistic variety* (Hudson 1996) when they want to be precise, as in "there is more than one (linguistic) variety spoken in our center." This avoids what could become a frivolous debate about whether someone speaks one language or two, signs, or uses a dialect, patois, or creole. Categorizing someone's speech matters less than what people do or mean as they communicate. In real life, language practices are dynamic because they make creative use of cultural systems that involve translators, agents, sponsors, gestures, and various workarounds to overcome linguistic and cultural barriers. At some point, language transcends itself, which has led some scholars to posit *pluralingualism* (Canagarajah 2009) or *translingualism* (Huang

2010; Schwarzer et al. 2006) as a way to describe the processes for exercising communicative competence in linguistically diverse settings. Whereas *multilingualism* refers to a state or goal, *translingualism* refers to efforts to reach beyond the limits of any single language and thus create communication bridges—along with detours, tunnels, and overpasses—that compel cooperation through communication. "Bilingual people translanguage as they make meaning in speech communities that are, in the twenty-first century, no longer attached to a national territory, and thus to a single national language," observes Ofelia García (2010, 199). García does not mean that bilingual people no longer identify with their mother tongues or feel strong attachment to the languages they have learned. Nor is the investment a person makes in learning a language somehow diminished (see García, Kleifgen, and Falchi, 2008). Quite the opposite is true. As Horner, Lu, and Matsuda (2010) have shown in *Cross-Language Relations in Composition*, the steps people take to communicate by reaching across linguistic barriers take on greater significance when the world shrinks because they are less beholden to the sense of identity they derive from a single language and more invested in what they can accomplish with multiple languages.

For directors and all literacy educators, it is important to resist efforts that isolate rather than integrate ethnolinguistically diverse people because English, despite its dominance, is still like every other language—a player in the mix of linguistic codes and more a means for achieving goals than an end in itself. Moreover, and as with any language, speaking and writing in English mean using certain varieties of the language over others, and these varieties have consequences. When tutors work with multilingual writers, we usually expect them to be able to deal with the question of how much deviation from standard edited English instructors will tolerate. As Aya Matsuda and Paul Kei Matsuda (2010) explain, "Every time L2 writers write in English, they are engaging in a language-contact situation. To prepare students adequately in the era of globalization, we as teachers need to fully embrace the complexity of English and facilitate the development of global literacy" (373). Tutors cannot assume teachers have embraced these values, but there are ways for them to understand the tensions that surround students' use of one variety or another in their writing. Matsuda and Matsuda suggest five useful principles for tutors to bear in mind:

1. Teach the dominant language forms and functions—in other words, proffer the codes that expand a client's options in education and life.

2. Teach the nondominant language forms and functions, or the deviations and what they signify.

3. Teach the boundary between what works and what doesn't— that is, variety is usually welcome, but not error.

4. Teach the principles and strategies of discourse negotiation— the rhetorical situatedness of writing, including audience, purpose, and genre.

5. Teach the risks involved in using deviational features. (Matsuda and Matsuda 2010, 373)

Another way for tutors to understand the dynamic nature of multilingualism is to consider the educational history of language users. Every person has learned to speak, write, read, and listen in ways that reveal the conditions that affected their learning and that are reflected in the speaking and writing they present in a writing conference. Dana Ferris (2009, 9–22) offers a useful list of descriptors for second-language writers, gleaned from various sources and based on the history and circumstances of the learner's youth and education.

(1) International student: One who is born and grows up in another country and comes to the U.S. to study usually at the undergraduate or graduate level, and who intends to return home when finished with school.

(2) Late-arriving resident student: One who plans to remain in the U.S. and comes to the country after age 10 and/or has been here for fewer than eight years.

(3) Early-arriving resident student: One who is born in the U.S. of immigrant parents, arrived before age 10, or has been in the country eight years or longer.

While *age, length of stay, adaptability, range of experience, family influence, long-term commitment,* and other terms are not used precisely in these definitions, they help to differentiate the conditions that influence how much and how quickly learners learn English. International students tend to have certain features in common that are a result of their schooling and home literacy from an early age. For example, they are generally aware of basic differences between orality and literacy, read and write in their L1, and draw upon their reading and writing experience as they learn *L2* literacy. They are probably successful as students because their families helped to support their education. Particularly in cases in which families have had to make sacrifices for their children's education, these students are often extremely dedicated to school.

In terms of acculturation, it is difficult to know the extent to which international students identify with the culture of their host country, and their identification can change. By definition, international students plan to return to their home countries, so their hearts are usually still at home with the friends and family they dearly miss. And yet they may also retain deep connections to their host universities and travel throughout the country before, during, and after their time in school. Moreover, regardless of their attitudes toward the host when they arrive, the extent to which they interact with students, faculty, and members of the community during their stay makes a tremendous difference in their well-being, happiness, and learning.

There are other ways to think about the circumstances behind the different levels of proficiency tutors see when multilingual students visit the writing center. Some may be considered *functional bilinguals* because they are using the language in a limited but more or less stable way, perhaps mainly in the context of a specific interest, trade, or skill. Many are considered *elective bilinguals* because they choose to learn English (or their parents make the choice for them); they may also be referred to as *additive bilinguals* because they opt to add English to their repertoire of languages. In contrast, *circumstantial bilinguals* have little choice but to learn English, which usually diminishes their use of the first language; they are sometimes called *subtractive bilinguals*. "Bilingual American minorities are, by definition, circumstantial bilinguals," says Guadalupe Valdés (1992). "They are forced by circumstances to acquire English, and they do so in a context in which their own first languages are accorded little or no prestige by the larger society" (94). One assumption behind these terms is that those who choose to learn a language are likely to be more invested in it, or to at least have more options, than those who are obliged to learn it or who use it mainly to function or get by. Despite these differences and depending on their personal and family histories, it is usually safe to assume that multilingual students who visit the writing center on their own are there because they are highly motivated to acquire advanced literacy in English. The advanced literacy they may already possess in their first language may be hard to see, but as they learn more English it will emerge. Their L1 literacy may not include much experience with types of writing we would recognize as critical or personal, but like any new form, these types of writing can be learned.

The terms above indicate the influence of conditions for learning and how language acquisition is affected by life's circumstances. For example, the labels *elective* and *functional* are insufficient to describe people who grew up surrounded by functional bilinguals and at a young age acquired certain non-English phonological features in their native speech. They are full-fledged bilinguals or English monolinguals, and not learners. Allan Metcalf (1979) refers to them as *contact bilinguals* and gives the example of Chicano English in Mexican American communities, which he describes as a variety of English spoken by "people whose native language is a special variety of English with a Spanish sound to it" (1). This example is yet another reason it is important for writing centers to try to get to know the students they serve, including something about their personal histories and present circumstances.

While international students in the United States are here mostly because they choose to study in the United States, many refugees and immigrants do not necessarily choose or want to learn English or any new language. Even some international students arriving in the United States for the first time, or feeling homesick and alone, experience some of the same feelings as those who have been forced to leave their homes. While it is true that these international students are able to return home, they may pay a huge price for doing so in terms of scholarship money they would have to repay and the shame they would bring to their families for not making it in college. These risks become a factor in the motivation students feel to improve while receiving tutoring in the writing center. Just as elective bilinguals possess a stronger need for advanced literacy in English, some immigrants or homesick international students may feel an aversion to being proficient in English, perhaps thinking greater proficiency in English diminishes their connection to their own heritage.

When international multilingual students enroll in a college or university in the United States, they are expected to know English well—to read, write, speak, and listen proficiently and across a range of disciplines: for example, intense reading and writing in a humanities class, straight lectures in biology, group work and discussions in business, nurse-patient interaction in a hospital internship. The expectations from one discipline, course, and instructor to another can vary so dramatically that a student who performs in a manner consistent with advanced speakers in one class can appear more limited in another. The risks and rewards language learners experience on a daily basis can be difficult for monolingual tutors to appreciate. Seen in this light, the fact that so many multilingual students read and write as well as they do is rather remarkable.

It is one thing to think about multilingual writers as international, late arriving, early arriving, elective, and functional and quite another to sit down with them to work on an assignment. Labels are often not a good fit when it comes to individuals because they can mislabel. This is true of the labels above, but also of other common labels such as *international, multi-*, and *second*, which tend to mask the individual's first or national identity. Labels like *ELL* or *learner* can mislabel, too, because they beg the question of when someone is fully proficient and no longer a learner. For example, is a mature adult who has worked in the United States for two decades and speaks with an accent an English *learner*? Labels with *English* or *language* (ESL, EAL— English as an additional language) tend to privilege English over other languages and emphasize the language over the person. In the abstract, these may not seem so serious, but when they are used to refer to actual individuals who don't fit the generalizations, they can be denigrating.

This problem of grouping students in various ways for educational purposes creates the kind of gap that linguist Adrian Holliday (1999) perceives between large and small cultures. In Holliday's view, "large culture" is associated with ethnicity, nationality, or internationality, while "small culture" is any cohesive social group. For the most part, the labels we use to name different types of learners align with notions of large culture. It is often necessary to speak about large-culture groups when examining, for example, broad social forces, especially from a historical perspective. The danger comes when we fail to make the shift from large-culture categories to small ones. For example, tutors may be inclined to see all students from one country or ethnic group as highly motivated, hardworking, and serious minded until they get to know individual members of this group and form more nuanced views about them. Students from other countries may consider all Americans to be part of the same large culture of, say, shopping and entertainment until they make friends with individual Americans.

While such notions may have the familiar ring of stereotyping, there are at least two less obvious points worth noting. One is that small-culture categories are far more dynamic than large-culture ones, and they are not easy to describe or predict. Classrooms are good examples: a community of learners comes together, bonds, creates its own expectations and conventions, and then disperses. The other point is that small-culture categories are not necessarily subsumed by large culture, like nested Russian dolls, as Holliday says. Instead, small culture can reach outside of large culture and be something beyond it, even as it exists in a place dominated by large culture. For example, a group of people may develop values, practices, and attitudes that have more in common with groups on another continent than with the groups they live among. The cohesiveness of such small-culture groups is the key to knowing and understanding them. Neither labels nor inferences are easily translated from large cultures to small ones.

A SISTERLY THING

Several decades ago, collaboration among peers, or the idea that students can help one another by working together toward a common goal, was borne of a need to bypass traditional academic hierarchies and the gate-keeping function of writing requirements (Bruffee 1999; Kail 1983; Kail and Trimbur 1987). Traditional, teacher-centered classrooms gave way to newer, student-centered pedagogies. Today, some of these same values that invigorated writing centers in the United States are making their way around the world and creating small cultures. Changes in education are rippling through schools and universities abroad, with some of the most dramatic reforms occurring in what are deemed traditional contexts. Saudi Arabia is an example. While it has a relatively high literacy rate and provides abundant support for education, traditional teaching methods prevail, and women and girls are held to strict behavioral codes. Yet the role of women and education in Saudi society is changing. A small measure of this change is thanks to the concept of writing centers imported from the United States.

For most of her career, Dr. Barbara Toth directed the writing center at Bowling Green State University in Ohio, United States, where she played host to international students in the campus writing center and in her home at the dining-room table. Several of her Saudi students wanted someone like Barbara in their country, and a few years ago she leaped at the opportunity to start a writing center at Princess Nora bint Abdul Rahman University in the nation's capital. With a new main campus built for forty thousand students and twelve thousand employees, Princess Nora University is the largest women-only university in the world. Toth navigated a foreign bureaucracy, educated tutors, and modeled the kind of collaborative work she expected of tutors and students, but that is something she had already done in the United States. What made this opportunity different was not only the students but also the necessarily multilingual setting.

Toth brought some of her Western ideas about teaching and learning to her new role, and she tried to explain to me why she finds the small culture, or local context, so meaningful in the place where she now lives and works: positive and negative features exist everywhere in the world, but they are not the same everywhere. For example, she was not surprised to find that her writers and tutors at PNU tended to view writing as an act of correction rather than one of discovery and change. But she also discovered that the notion of challenging beliefs under the aegis of critical thinking—a familiar posture for American tutors—can be seen as strange and offensive by the women students who visit and tutor in the PNU center. To understand this reaction it is necessary to define what critical thinking means in a context like the United States, and that <u>distinction</u> leads to the realization that definitions of the notion vary widely.

Women in Saudi society seem quite adept at one kind of critical thinking, Toth found, and it was one that did not come so easily to her undergraduate students in Ohio. She noticed that Saudi women students who visited PNU's writing center apprehended the concept of audience awareness quite readily, something she attributed, perhaps, to their multilingual positioning and the ease with which they go in and out of various social contexts. She points to the tradition of بلاغة (Arabic rhetoric) that is as familiar to these students as Western rhetoric is to Americans and Europeans. This kind of moving in and out of large and small cultures is relevant for understanding the rhetorical aspects of writing, Toth believes, and can be applied to one of her students' favorite writing assignments: how beloved King Abdullah is by his people. "They learn that when they write they have to think about audience: Who is asking the question?

Who will read what you write and what do they expect? What will interest them?" she explained. Within the large culture of their country and Muslim identity, these women enact a reverence for their leader at the same time they practice what seems like a Western rhetorical value for audience awareness.

Surprisingly, audience awareness isn't the only Western rhetorical idea they easily pick up. "Collaboration," Toth said, "they get it. Writing centers have great value here. My tutors love to coauthor, and they don't complain about one doing more work than another. They throw themselves into it. It's a sisterly thing." Today students have multiple ways to communicate with one another, but writing centers remain places where peers form relationships around their fields of study. When these relationships are created, the opportunities for learning are magnified because students learn from one another but also collaborate and compete with one another for recognition and rewards. The challenge for tutors and directors is to lead peer tutors to take the relationships that exist among themselves and with clients to a higher plane where more teaching and learning can occur. The challenge, in other words, is to raise our expectations for the goals that tutors and students can achieve. The kind of international work Toth is doing—the practices and values she has brought to students at PNU—are based on the small-culture understanding she has with her students. From a writing center to a dining-room table in northeast Ohio, and then on to a women's university in the heart of the Middle East, collaborative learning is nothing if not about the one-to-one.

Not long after she arrived at PNU, Barbara Toth set about connecting her tutors and their new writing center with the Middle East-North Africa Writing Centers Alliance (MENAWCA) regional organization. In 2012 she and her tutors traveled to MENAWCA's conference in Qatar to make presentations. A poster created by tutors Abeer Aloshan, Gadeer Alshahwan, Loujain Alghamdi, and Afnan Felmban on the topic of reconceptualizing tutoring toward a sustainable culture of writing reflected the seamlessness these tutors discovered between tutoring and friendship. It contains a Möbius strip marked with four principles—joy, trust, work, and balance—signifying stages the tutors believe they and their writers pass through when a session is effective.

On the other side of the globe from Riyadh is Bronx Community College. Yadira (not her name) is an undergraduate tutor there who considers Urdu and Bangla (Bengali) her first languages. In the home where she grew up, English was spoken as well. Yadira has thought about the languages she knows and what she has been able to offer students in her three years of tutoring, and she has decided that empathy is the most important thing.

> First, I introduce myself and I get to know them—classes they're taking, and so on. I ask them, did you have lunch? Is the temperature okay? I try to get them talking. I say, "Tell me some good things about your country."
>
> I really want to make sure they learn something, you know? I look at them and I ask, "Are you willing?" You have to get them to commit, because it's hard. Yes. But first, I get to know them.

Yadira seems to understand something that eludes most new tutors: putting students at ease and asking them if they are comfortable is one thing, but challenging and motivating them to work hard, and work smarter, is another. She sets high expectations for writers. Not all tutors can pull this off, and it's understandable. Setting high expectations for others means doing the same for oneself.

I also spoke with Penelope Meyers, another tutor at BCC. She learned French in Malawi, where she was born, and grew up in Washington, DC, and Malawi. Meyers has a bachelor's degree in comparative literature. When I asked her to describe an ideal tutor, she stressed conscientiousness and knowing "where the student is" in every moment of the session. "What I mean is, I would want a tutor who is engaged, not one who is sitting back, and not someone who is talking all the time either." She continued, "I'd like a partner, someone who is really listening to me and not trying to push over me. A partner in the process." Careful listening is often overlooked. Addressing tutors directly, Paul Matsuda and Michelle Cox (2009) offer this advice about listening: "When we listen—truly listen—we treat ESL writers with the respect they deserve, regarding them as peers rather than as uninformed learners of English language and the U.S. culture. It is only in such an atmosphere of mutual respect that the collaborative pedagogy of the writing center can turn differences into opportunities for growth both for the reader and the writer" (49).

Tutors and the students they work with are increasingly multilingual and multicultural in their orientations toward academic literacy. Twenty years ago, the values in American writing centers seemed to be firmly aligned with native English speakers and the monolingual culture they grew up in. These values prevail in some places, but they are changing. Today, multilingual writers are inside the tent and moving the center pole, asserting greater control over the use of English and what it means to them. Increasingly, writing centers are places where multilingual writers see language less as an end in itself and more as a means to achieving what they want *to do*, like sharing an experience, building relationships, and making a life for themselves and others.

2

LEARNING FROM INTERACTION

Tutors and teachers tend to judge a consultation or class by how engaged they feel when they are in it. A good class is lively and time flies. A boring class is one in which nobody talks but the teacher. These generalizations don't give a complete picture, however, because engagement in teaching and learning has many facets. It's not a matter of who does the talking or how much talking there is; an interesting lecture can be more stimulating than a plodding discussion, for example. Acquiring a deeper understanding of notions like interaction is important for tutors because engagement (generally) and interaction (in particular) are the lifeblood of learning. People's in-the-moment feelings of interaction with what is going on around them increase when they begin to pay attention to others and the environment. What someone learns and takes away from the experience often depends on how long this feeling can be sustained. It also depends on what is meant by interaction. People can be riveted by experiences that may seem passive outwardly, like reading a novel or an in-depth investigative report, listening to a famous speaker or musical performance, or viewing a landscape or work of art. Experiences like these can make viewers and listeners feel engaged or involved, even though they may appear to be passive on the outside. To say that there is interaction, however, means that people are communicating back and forth. The many facets of interaction span a range of thoughts and actions, which is why interaction is not only essential to learning generally but to learning language specifically. And the more this interaction also involves a positive relationship, the better.

DOI: 10.7330/9780874219647.c002

TUTORING AND RELATIONSHIPS

Paulina, a tutor at the University of Manitoba, told me about her first visits to the writing center when she was a freshman and shortly after she had moved with her family from El Salvador to Canada, having studied English in school since fourth grade: "I went to the writing center to help me with my papers. It was really useful. I really liked one tutor who would help me with words. He was really friendly and I could relate to him. I learned from the interaction." Being immersed in English for the first time hastened Paulina's language acquisition, but the writing center stands out in her mind, especially the opportunity for social interaction and conversation. She had thought her English was really good when she arrived in Canada, but she seriously underestimated how much more she needed to learn: "When we left home to come here, I had just finished high school. But my dad made me enroll in twelfth grade here anyway. I was so mad. I was really opposed to this," she said ruefully. "A teenager, you know. Now, I'm glad I did it and wish I had learned even more from that year."

Paulina has now graduated with a degree in psychology and will begin graduate studies in psychology and public health at Carleton University. But as a new arrival six years ago and a long way from her Spanish roots, learning to converse in English and making friends were as important to Paulina as anything the writing center had to offer. At the beginning of her senior year, Paulina became a tutor in the center. "It was around this time that I began to think in English for the first time, so that was only about a year ago. That's when I realized it," she said. Paulina's experience reflects part of what Brian Fallon (2010) has called the lived, perceived, and conceived experiences of tutoring. Tutors come to us as individuals living their own histories, needs, and desires. They are also perceived through particular lenses—by other tutors, in the literature of the field, by directors, and so on. And they can be conceived in ways that have not yet been fully realized or imagined. Paulina told me her tutor had a big impact on her adjustment to life and language in Canada, even though she shared little of that part of her story in the interview. Paulina and her tutor became partners and learned from interacting with each other in ways that are possible only between peers.

In research conducted for his doctoral dissertation, Fallon (2010) documented how tutors do what they think is possible to help writers in a given situation. He studied something that Barbara Toth and her tutors at PNU might think of as their "sisterly thing"—the comfort level tutors and writers feel significantly influences what is possible for them to achieve. He concluded that "relationships in the writing center are also tied to the ways that tutors establish trust, goodwill, and confidence in their interactions with writers and to some extent with other tutors" (195). Fallon's study steps back to contemplate the various roles the field of writing centers has assigned to tutors and concludes that these can never be fixed because teaching and learning never stay the same. Fallon writes, "While many scholars worked to establish a kind of institutional role for tutors (i.e., 'big students,' 'little teachers,' 'interpreters,' 'organic intellectuals'), the fact remains that the educational role and the job of peer tutors will probably always be in a constant state of revision" (Fallon 2010, 225–26). The job of peer tutors today is, in fact, being revised as it is knitted into the fabric of global education for students who have traveled great distances when they walk into a writing center in the United States.

Since he was six years old, Antoine Dahdah Sayegh had attended a private school to learn English. "My mother sacrificed a lot so I could attend this school," he told me. He continued to talk about what he likes to write about when he uses the language his mother sacrificed for. "I am very thankful for my family and what they have done for me. I like to write about my values and what I have done so far in my life. I want people to value me for who I am." Antoine is now studying business and finance at Nova Southeastern University. When he sits down for a consultation at the campus writing center, his tutor may or may not know his story, but Antoine never forgets the obligation he feels to his mother and other members of his family. Adults tend to learn a second, third, or fourth language out of necessity or passion; it is too difficult to do for any other reason. For many, English is a means to attain social mobility, cultural and personal enrichment, and a path out of poverty, isolation, and tedious labor. Tutors are not usually aware of these factors, but they need to know that motivation, resourcefulness, will power, and even strong feelings of guilt, honor, and obligation may lie just beneath the surface in a consultation. For people like Antoine, learning English is as much about the sacrifices his family made to create a better life for him as it is about his own ambition.

In a center where there are multilingual tutors, at some point the topic of writers who prefer to work with native English-speaking tutors comes up. The issue can manifest itself subtly in appointment patterns, for instance, or candidly if a writer says up front that they want to work only with one of the "English-speaking" tutors. The roots of this bias are somewhat different for monolingual and multilingual writers. Multilingual writers may be transferring a bias from language schools in the countries where they grew up and where the best English teachers are often considered to be native speakers because it is believed they know best the correct grammar and pronunciation of English. Jessica Williams (2008) found that the L2 writers in her study benefitted regardless of whether or not tutors had explicit knowledge of English grammar. Terese Thonus (2012) concludes that tutors' interactional skills for deriving grammar rules prove to be more important than their explicit knowledge of grammar. Multilingual writers may also want native-speaking tutors in the hope the tutors will remove from the student's writing any trace of accent so their papers scan for the kind of native-like *idiomaticity* many learners desire.

This last point is an important one for directors and tutors to discuss; a classic article by Valdés (1992) provides a good foundation for understanding the many reasons native-like idiomaticity remains an elusive goal. They include the nature of learning a first versus another language, the contexts in which languages are learned and the models for usage, and the individual's own predispositions and attitudes. They also include the expectation of many teachers and members of American society that there is only one correct way to speak and write English and that every student in school must be held accountable for mastering the correct way. Valdés explains the reasons this expectation is not supported by research.

From a tutor's perspective, the issue of native-like idiomaticity often arises when an advanced writer, perhaps a graduate student, presents writing that is well written but not fully native sounding, or idiomatic. The tutor sees only a few grammatical errors but otherwise recognizes phrases that are not expressed exactly the way a native speaker would write them and senses a hard-to-define or accented quality to the writing. Normally this quality would not be a problem except that the writer wants the paper to be both grammatically perfect and free from traces of his accent, which may be marked, for example, by the occasional usage or omission of articles and prepositions that seems slightly off. This situation can leave tutors in a quandary: on the one hand, there are places in the paper that don't sound quite right. On the other hand, tutors are the only ones who can fix them and in fact feel it may be their duty to do so, or at least to help.

The phenomenon of *native-speaker privilege* (Phillipson 1992), also known as native-speaker fallacy, native speakerism (Holliday 2005, 2006), and idealized native speaker (Leung et al. 1997) is a phenomenon with deep cultural roots and broad effects in cultural identity and education. Although every language has native speakers, the phenomenon of native-speaker privilege is most widespread when it comes to English because of English's global dominance. It helps to explain why many English speakers feel little need to learn other languages and relish their English-language identity, even mythologizing it as somehow special or unique (see Rafoth 2009 for a fuller discussion on this topic). Native-speaker privilege also helps explain why people in many places of the world who aspire to learn English defer to native speakers whose skin color is white. Pei-hsun Emma Liu (2010) found that Taiwanese college students in her study developed an identity of inferiority when learning English composition in Taiwan, a phenomenon she attributed to their adoption of a culturally conditioned white prestige ideology. They also displayed resistance when they felt their teachers did not teach Standard English and other conventions, thus slowing their access to white prestige. She wrote:

> Most Taiwanese students in my research constructed an identity of inferiority in their English composition classes because of their white prestige and native-speaker ideology. They felt unconfident in their English composition and viewed their writing teachers as legitimate correctors. Thus, they viewed themselves as inferior goods waiting for opportunities to upgrade. Taiwanese writers accommodated or resisted teaching instruction to invest in the imagined community of prestige so that they could enjoy social capital and higher social status. They gained superficial empowerment when investing in the imagined community of prestige. (Liu 2010, 218)

Native-speaker privilege often accounts for why some international students—and some native English-speaking students—avoid tutors who are not native English speakers. As it diminishes every other language, the ideology of native-speaker privilege elevates native speakers' power and sense of superiority over those who feel othered by it. For purposes of international trade, culture, and book publishing, native-speaker privilege hegemonizes English and makes it hard for postcolonial Englishes to gain legitimacy. The linguistic landscape is changing, however, as communities claim authority over their use of indigenous and local varieties in places like South Africa (Peirce 1989), Sri Lanka (Canagarajah 1993), the Caribbean (Irvine and Elsasser 1988), and elsewhere.

The issue of writers who want to nativize their writing is a good discussion to have with tutors unfamiliar with the concept of native-speaker privilege. Molly Wingate's (2005) warning against providing too much help to writers provides a starting point for tutors because it emerges from monolingual assumptions. Does the warning still apply when working with multilingual writers? Before asking how much help a tutor should provide, it pays to consider the writer's level of proficiency, the kind of help being asked for, and the purpose for writing. Advanced multilingual writers whose meaning is clear and who are working on achieving idiomaticity in their writing can benefit from a native speaker's intuitions and corrections because those writers have become so proficient in English that they are ready to take on the finer points of style and usage learned mainly from experience and feedback.

Before going down that road, though, tutors must be prepared to recognize accented writing as a choice the writer has made. In other words, tutors must consider the possibility that writers have decided their English is probably good enough and do not want, or need to make it sound like someone they are not. On the other hand, writers still struggling to produce well-formed sentences and to select accurate words require, more than anything else, a tutor who can help them to prioritize these matters, and that tutor may well be multilingual. Preparation of tutors and the director's influence are critical.

There is also a gray area that most language teachers acknowledge: sometimes circumstances warrant simply telling the writer how to express an idea idiomatically in the target language. Doing so may be necessary under some circumstances, such as when

- writers have a clear sense of the idea and how to express it in their first language but do not understand how to say it in English. Tutors have a responsibility to help the writer find a way, and if both share the same first language, then shifting into it can provide both a cognitive and motivational bridge back to English. Crystal Mitchell, a Spanish-English bilingual tutor, said, "Spanish is my first language and Natasha and I are in the same class. I can explain something to her in Spanish and she understands it so much better because in Spanish, it seems so much stronger—there's so much more passion. And because it's my first language, I feel so much more confidence when I explain it";
- the writer has attempted to put the idea into words but the phrasing is so ill formed and potentially embarrassing that it begs for the tutor's recasting;
- the writer needs to overcome a small problem of mixed-up words in order to begin to address a larger and more important problem;

- or sometimes when exhausted writers just want to know
  (without always having to justify their request), "How would
  you say this?" In this case, it is worth remembering that tutoring is built on a relationship. Instead of worrying that writers
  are looking for a crutch, it is more productive to trust that
  they are being diligent, gathering pieces of language and
  putting them together at their own pace.

Giving a writer "the answer" to a minor problem in order to
move on to something more important—or just to move on—
will strike some directors and tutors as wrong because it means
giving words to students that are not strictly their own. They
may feel it is never appropriate for a tutor to cross this line, or
that once they have crossed it, the line will continue to erode
(Wingate 2005). But as Barbara Toth observed (personal communication), writers often do not have the *emicity* to easily separate less from more important problems. By *emicity* she means
the ability to distinguish differences (in wording, grammar, and
so on) that matter from differences that don't. For this reason,
writers may remain fixated on a minor point that effectively
wastes a lot of time and never get around to problems that
are more serious—not because they are lazy but because their
English proficiency is not yet advanced enough. When tutors
step in and help writers to reorient away from something minor
and toward a major point, they provide an opportunity for
learning that would otherwise be lost. It is worth recalling that
instead of barking "look it up" as teachers used to do in the old
days, teachers today try to spell words when a student asks for
help because they realize it's important to help a writer move on
to the next word. Besides, withholding a piece of information
can come across as petty.

On the question of automatically deferring to a writer's
request to be assisted by a native English-speaking consultant,
one way to address this issue is to begin a discussion among
tutors and directors about people's attitudes toward prestige
versus stigmatized varieties of language. A good place to begin
is with Paul Matsuda's (2006) description of the "myth of linguistic homogeneity," or the mistaken belief that Americans

speak only one language (see also Jordan 2012; Lu and Horner 2013; Trimbur 2010). When it comes to urging writers to consider the reasons a multilingual tutor may be the best match for them, this discussion is probably best handled by tutors who have discussed the matter with their director ahead of time and are prepared to address it with the writer. Related to the myth of linguistic homogeneity is Canagarajah's (2005) perspective.

> A repertoire of variant dialects is important for many today to be functional in the post-modern world. Rather than developing a mastery of a specific code, students need the interactional skills to negotiate dialect differences with their interlocutors. For this purpose, an awareness of diverse dialects is a resource that should be educationally validated. Rather than teaching standard dialects one-sidedly, it might be more important to develop a repertoire of dialects—with an awareness of their values, structure, and their contextual appropriateness in different situations. (941)

Instead of immediately complying with a student's request for a specific tutor, or worse, dismissing it, tutors and directors should be aware of the reasons behind that request and be prepared to encourage the student to try a different option.

NEGOTIATED INTERACTION

Theory and research on the role of *negotiated interaction* in second-language learning span decades, and one thing they show consistently is that the back and forth of conversation is not merely an opportunity to practice using the language but is itself a source of learning (Gass and Varonis 1985; Long 1981; 1983). The main benefit of negotiated interaction is that it enables the simultaneous focus on form and meaning. A number of second-language researchers have examined negotiated interaction in tutoring sessions and reached a similar conclusion (Daiute and Dalton 1985; Thompson 2009). Terese Thonus (2004) studied native-nonnative speakers' interactions and found that native English-speaking tutors tended to speak more often and control the session more when they were tutoring nonnative English speakers. They also negotiated less and referred the writers back to their instructors more than they did with NES writers. Jennifer Ritter and Tyrgve Sandvik (2009) show how tutors respond to Generation 1.5 students, who tend to have good oral fluency but relatively weak skills for academic writing and reading due mainly to the oral conditions in which they learned English. Ritter and Sandvik's work illustrates how an assignment that involves reading a text closely requires tutors to question and guide a Generation 1.5 writer's attention more than an international student's.

Conversations with native as well as nonnative speakers are one of the most effective ways to learn another language, but does *any* kind of conversational interaction with a tutor benefit language learning, or are some types more helpful than others? If some are more helpful, then what do they look like and how can those be encouraged? Alister Cumming and Sufumi So (1996) found that when tutors' and writers' interactions revolve around a shared vocabulary for revision, writers are better able to "identify, negotiate, or resolve problems in their writing" (207). When we think about how crucial it is for second-language students to participate in a shared vocabulary, and the central role of conversation in the foundations of peer tutoring (Bruffee 1999), it is clear that there is a lot to learn about the kinds of interactions we want conversations to bring about. Conversations happen so naturally that there is a tendency to let them take care of themselves, but in fact tutors need to learn about effective conversational interactions, as does anyone in a helping profession for whom talk is the primary instrument, including negotiators, counselors, and clinicians.

Often overlooked in interactive communication is the importance of listening. Listening well is hard under the best of circumstances, but it can be a huge challenge for second-language learners. For those who learned English through lots of oral/aural interaction in natural settings—with friends, at work, in daycare—listening has been a part of their lives and will continue to play a major role in their interactions. For many international students, by contrast, English was learned through formal English-language classes, similar to the way American students study Spanish or German in school; for them, listening was probably not as important as reading and reciting. As a broad generalization, then, international students tend to have an instruction-based L2-language-learning experience in school, while early- and late-arriving residents have a more conversation-based experience. Again, though, this is a generalization. Exceptions include international students who traveled to English-speaking countries as they were learning the language, students whose parents may have immigrated to America and begun speaking English to their young children, or the international student whose English class was taught in an immersion setting.

The difference between these groups can be significant and is known informally among ESL teachers as *ear learners* versus *eye learners,* terms coined by Joy Reid (2011). While the dichotomy is an oversimplification, the point is that *how* people learn a second language makes a difference in how well prepared they are to use the language in some contexts versus others. "Languages are conceived and languaging is practiced," writes Walter Mignolo (1996, 1). The practice of language for ear learners means that they absorb much of what they know by listening and from their day-to-day experiences in natural settings; for example, they have probably experienced a good deal of trial and error in speaking situations, and for this reason they tend to be more comfortable with taking risks, repairing mistakes, and the overall back and forth of spontaneous speech than their eye-learner counterparts. They are probably also good at using the full range of conversational pragmatics—things like nodding (to indicate active listening or agreement) and moving their heads slightly (to indicate they didn't hear or understand). Eye learners, on the other hand, take in much of what they know by reading books. They used English mainly in recitations and likely did not learn to navigate their way around spontaneous extended conversations. Their speech may be heavily accented. They may also be uncomfortable making mistakes, admitting they don't understand, or asking for help.

Natascha is a tall, athletic undergraduate who plays on Nova University's golf team and may be classified as an eye learner.

She was born in Venezuela and had been in the United States for one year when I met her in 2012. Natascha did well in school as a writer but said she has a hard time in some speaking situations. She explained:

> It's very hard to improvise, to come up with something. For example, if you're doing a presentation and you forget something it's not easy to start speaking about something else, in your own way. You need to memorize stuff because you cannot express yourself. It's not like your common sense saves you— you're speaking another language and you start feeling nervous, stuttering, and not making sense. So you have to memorize things.

She recalled speaking in front of the class without notes.

> I took a public-speaking class and had to give a demonstration speech. I tried to show the class how to make a putting stroke, like in miniature golf, you know? I thought it was going to be so easy. But when I was in front of people I was nervous so I wasn't thinking straight and I find it difficult when I wanted to say how to grab the club. I knew it in Spanish, but I just said, "uhm, uhm" and thought, "What am I gonna do?"

She laughed as she told this story, but I could see it wasn't so funny for her at the time because here she was, talking about the one thing, a putting stroke, that she knew better than anybody else in the class. She confided, "For my next speech, I just wrote it in Spanish, translated everything, memorized it so I wouldn't have that problem. It's so hard. It's like, 'What am I gonna do if I mess it up?'"

In tutoring sessions, ear learners would seem to have an advantage when it comes to listening because they have developed conversation skills. They are likely to pick up on a tutor's intonational cues and to recognize humor, sarcasm, and colloquial and slang expressions. They often seem more confident and at ease when they sit down to talk. Because of their experience using spoken English, their colloquial usage and accurate pronunciation may lead tutors to think they are also proficient writers in English. Tutors may be surprised, however, to find that the ear learner they are working with does not have a very good academic vocabulary and, unlike eye learners, is not as familiar with the conventions of written texts, such as macro organizers like "as we will see in the next section," "in sum," "more to the point," and so on.

Tutors have a special responsibility to be authentic listeners, Gemma Corradi Fiumara (1990) reminded: "Authentic listening occurs only when 'an embryonic thought is protected from the restrictive interference of over-zealous classification'" (Fiumara 1990, ctd. in Grimm 1999, 53). Classifications like ear learner and eye learner are useful for describing tendencies pertaining to the experiences of learning English and their effects on current performance, but they are overly simplified categories and not appropriate for classifying all multilingual writers. Tutors must be authentic listeners, listening not only for what they expect to hear but also for what they don't. Most of all, they need to be ready to respond to the writer, one human being to another. Recognizing these opportunities for response is something writing centers should excel at.

LEARNING ONE'S FIRST LANGUAGE AND THEN ANOTHER

As we saw above, how someone learns a language affects what they can do with it. Someone who learns a language from early childhood has a number of advantages over someone who tries to learn it later in life. Much the same holds true for literacy and learning to write. This is one reason it is important to examine second-language writing from a somewhat different perspective than learning to write in one's first language—"somewhat" because there are both similarities and differences between the two. First- and second-language writers go through many of the same composing processes: they both juggle audience and purpose, and they have to learn field- and genre-specific conventions. Still, their differences cannot be overlooked.

For example, comparing the following conditions hints at some of the reasons learning to write in a second language is a different experience, and has different outcomes, for everyone:

- learning one's first language in the home with lots of exposure to interesting reading materials, including children's stories and bedtime reading;
- learning a second language primarily from playmates and older children;
- learning a foreign language in school, starting at a young age;
- learning a new language as a teenager in a place where that language is dominant.

Whether one learns in the home or at school, has easy access to reading materials or does not, or lives in a place where the target language is dominant or is not—these and other conditions affect how rapidly and how well a person is able to learn to write in a second language. Tutors who get to know the writers they work with may gain insight into the conditions that affected students' language learning. In the first condition above, and unlike the second, the learner probably has a good foundation of literacy to build on when working on a college-level writing assignment. In the third condition, although starting at a young age, the student's exposure to the new language is mainly through language classes, not real-life uses. In the fourth condition, learners start to learn when they are older but have the benefit of exposure to real-life uses of the language. There are trade-offs at every turn.

In terms of background knowledge, it is helpful for tutors to be aware of some of the differences between learning a second versus learning a first language. One of the most striking differences may be seen in the early years, when children follow roughly the same developmental sequence regardless of their specific language. Unless they have a developmental disability, virtually all children are able to discriminate between sounds long before they are able to produce them. They can produce upwards of fifty words by age two and use basic features of grammar; for example, English-speaking two- to three-year-olds know that *baby kiss* and *kiss baby* mean different things. By age six or so, children everywhere have learned most of the basic grammar of their first language and know how to ask questions, give commands, use negation, and take turns (Berko Gleason 2005).

They continue to learn new words every day and to expand their ability to use language in different situations. Second-language learners, by contrast, have already learned how to ask questions, give commands, and so on in their first language, and therefore many of their pragmatic skills transfer to their second language. Learning to use idioms, collocations, and cultural knowledge, on the other hand, must be learned over time through experience and practice. Tutors are a valuable resource for this learning.

When it comes to college, multilingual writers have different needs than monolingual writers. Multilingual writers may be accomplished, even published, writers in their L1. As a tutor from the University of Illinois's Writers Workshop, John O'Connor, pointed out, while this literacy affords them a distinct advantage, they may also feel particularly self-conscious about the difficulties of writing in their L2 and hold themselves to the same high standards they apply to writing in their L1. For tutors, strategies that seem natural with L1 writers may be counterproductive with L2 writers. All students struggle with writing, for example, but when given the opportunity, L1 writers can usually talk out their ideas as a bridge to getting thoughts down on paper. For less proficient second-language learners, however, talking out ideas also requires thinking about using the language: selecting the right words, forms, and pronunciations. These choices require concentration and therefore limit the ability to focus on verbalizing lots of ideas. Put another way, it is much more difficult for most L2 writers to simply say something without also thinking about how to say it. For this reason, asking an L2 writer who is struggling to put thoughts on paper for the purpose of talking it out is not the same as asking an L1 writer to do the same thing. This difference doesn't mean tutors should never ask L2 writers to think aloud, only that it depends on writers' levels of proficiency and comfort with the situation; if they say they are okay doing it, then that is probably the gauge to go by.

Learning to write in a second language is affected by writing instruction in and out of school. In the case of someone who is older and an immigrant, learning to speak or write in a second language can be significantly harder because adult immigrants, compared with young immigrants, often have more complex lives and responsibilities that make the monumental task of learning another language all the more difficult. This difficulty can be significantly lessened by frequent interactions with speakers of the new language, being in school, and taking advantage of tutoring, counseling, free classes, and other services—but access to these services is limited and not really feasible for many people. Being uprooted from one's homeland to settle in another country and make a new life there can be extraordinarily hard even for those who have the resources and good luck to avoid stress and hardships. Tutors are in a position to make this transition a little easier by attending closely to what students who come to the writing center need.

WORKING WITH THE WRITER

Interaction and the conditions for learning make a difference, but so does the way the mind works to store and process language. Interaction, conditions, and cognition intersect with each other. One can imagine this relationship in the abstract, or hear and see it in the words and eyes of language learners. Listening to these individuals as I did when interviewing them, one hears a passion for the intellectual work of language learning that involves diligence, concentration, and focus. It is a passion born of necessity, and it is often grounded in the mundane labor of continuous practice, feedback, setbacks, and small steps forward.

Amanda Amionne speaks with the quiet assurance of an old soul though she is in her early twenties. She holds her hands in her lap and frames her remarks in clear and cogent sentences, saying no more than needed but always saying plenty. She is a serious student. When asked, "What advice do you have for tutors who work with multilingual writers like yourself?" she says:

> Tutors have to work with the writer. They really have to be hands on —it's not like you give them something and they work on it. I think that's the only way it will stick because when you're young, it's easier. But when you're older and have to adapt to a whole

new language, it is so much harder for them. So if you want to teach them something, you have to stay with them. It should be something that's really intensive.

Asked if she likes intensity, she replies, "I think that's the only way to learn." Amanda is one of the brightest and most respected tutors in the Nova Writing Center, and her preferred way of tutoring sounds demanding, setting high expectations by working collaboratively and rewarding achievement. This approach may seem familiar enough, but what might tutoring sessions look and feel like in a writing center where intensity is common, part of the culture? To US tutors, it might evoke the atmosphere of a study floor at midterm in the university library. To some Koreans, a writing center with intense tutoring sessions might conjure up notions of *hagwon*, or cram schools, where parents enroll their children to learn English in expensive, privately owned and operated schools; children attend their regular school during the day and then take additional classes in the late afternoon, evening, or late into the night. Instruction includes lots of written exercises, recitations, books to read, and endless exams, by which the success of students and the schools are measured.

Hagwon is probably not what Amanda has in mind. International students who know of or have experience with *hagwon* nearly all hate them because students live and die by the tests used to mark progress and advance students to the next level. According to an article in the *Guardian* (de Lotbinière, Nov. 8, 2011), an interest group in South Korea has recently begun trying to persuade parents that cram schools before a certain age do more harm than good. They want parents to forego enrolling their children in English-language classes until their children are ten years old and can take advantage of immersion opportunities, where their children will learn English better and faster.

Leaving aside all the harmful ways to educate students, writing center tutors and directors also need to acknowledge the deep desire many students have for tough intellectual challenges, creative engagement, and clear signs of their productivity and accomplishment. How are writing centers designed to meet the needs of these students? One can imagine a writing center where tutors are held to high standards because they are well prepared to assist multilingual students, and where so-so tutoring doesn't cut it. Such writing centers might be places where tutors are put through a rigorous preparation course, observed, and given regular feedback on their sessions. A criterion for employment might be to know or study another language, or to minor in linguistics. And student work that currently earns praise for "good effort!" ("excellent!" "super!") might instead be met with responses like "try again." Instead of sessions lasting thirty to fifty minutes, they might last two hours and be led by an expert or master tutor working in concert with teams of tutors.

This environment is not the right one for every writing center, but the point is that many students who are highly motivated and smart crave this type of challenging learning environment and seek it out in their choices of majors and outside activities. Writing center directors and tutors could accommodate them better by reflecting on the expectations they set for these and all students. Amanda described her most intense moments of learning as occurring when she draws, alone in her studio, for three to four hours at a stretch. Writing, like drawing, involves creativity, focus, and discipline, and yet most writing centers that limit sessions to thirty to forty minutes do not seem geared toward cultivating these qualities.

Many tutors find their choice of instruction methods comes from what they themselves would like a tutor to tell them. Ariana Fonseca is also a multilingual tutor at Nova and said this about her own writing:

> Don't be afraid to say what is wrong in my essay. Don't be afraid to tell me. Is it the proper way, or is it just acceptance? I cannot accept that. They should say, write this way, it sounds more English. I can write something and they say, "Yeah, okay, I understand." But no. I need to start writing properly. They should not be ashamed to telling the true things.

Ariana may sound like a voice from a bygone era when school was meant to be arduous and even painful. In fact, many schools around the world still adhere to this approach, and Ariana's and Amanda's ideas about learning may reflect the schools they remember, much as some American college students learned, growing up, to expect trophies for participation. And yet Ariana and Amanda are accomplished multilingual tutors who have a broad range of educational experiences and an enviable level of spoken and written proficiency. Their perspective is worth getting to know better because it reflects a restlessness, a sense that a college education must do more for students. The question is, what are writing center directors doing to listen to students, tutors, and faculty about what students need and want to take on?

Kenisha Thomas has coordinated evening services in the writing center at Bronx Community College since 2008; she began as a tutor there five years before that. When asked what she wants her tutors to remember when they sit down to help writers, she spoke about students' needs.

> Students have ideas, whether well expressed or not. So they come to the writing center because they feel vulnerable. They come here because it's a safe place. Tutors learn to become compassionate, patient. Students open up and are vulnerable. We have to meet them where they are.

All tutors bring up the need to take the time and work with writers on a deeper level to achieve the writers' goals. Daniel Tehrani taught English in Turkey for a while before starting graduate school at Hunter College. He now works as a tutor and part-time instructor at Bronx Community College. He talked about working with writers and trying to figure out where to begin.

> Say I'm trying to learn Spanish. I would want somebody who could teach me about the language through grammar. I'd also want somebody who would not talk about grammar when I didn't want to do that, somebody who would not assume I want grammar just because I'm an NNS. That's key. A lot of times, NNSs can't express themselves well enough to say, "That's not what I want. What I want is . . ." On the other hand, they don't always know what they need—they can't do a needs assessment

of themselves. They just come in with a paper and say, "I need help with grammar." They're not sure what that means. The exception is maybe students who have a very high standard of academic literacy and know what grammar means and they really do want grammar. But they're coming from a different place.

Tutors like Daniel, Ariana, and Amanda are hard workers who see a side of students and writing that monolingual English-speaking tutors do not usually see because learning a new language is both exhilarating and exhausting. This is why US writing centers need diverse staffs that include multilingual writers and conversations about how we learn to speak and write.

MISCOMMUNICATION

The idea that miscommunication promotes language learning is counterintuitive for most people. Communicating clearly is supposed to be the goal, and yet miscommunication promotes growth in acquiring a second language, too. Miscommunication comes in different varieties, and it is not always beneficial for learning. For example, a simple misunderstanding can usually be cleared up with a bit of explanation.

Caller: Do I need an appointment to see a tutor?

Receptionist: No, you can just walk in.

Caller: I'd like to make an appointment.

Receptionist: Oh, sorry. I meant, we do not take appointments.

Caller: Okay, I'll come back when I'm ready then. Thanks.

Simple misunderstandings (Gass and Varonis 1991) like the one in this exchange usually involve an utterance or statement meant one way but taken another. Such brief exchanges may help learners to practice what they know, but they are not usually long or engaging enough to significantly enhance learning. Compare the spare conversation above to the complex one in the excerpt below.

This excerpt comes from Jennifer Ritter's (2002) doctoral dissertation and is one of many tutorials she observed in the writing center at Indiana University of Pennsylvania. In this excerpt, the tutor is trying to figure out what the writer means by the phrase *country fashion*. What the writer intends by it is not clear, exactly, and her instructor had marked it as awkward on her paper. When the writer calls the tutor's attention to the phrase, a negotiated interaction begins. The writer (female) is Korean and a first-year undergraduate. The tutor (female) is an American native-English speaker and a second-year undergraduate.

A note on the transcription is helpful here because some readers may want to try reading the transcript aloud to appreciate its richness. Ritter uses **boldface** to highlight elements for analysis, and I retained the boldface. The other devices I retained in her transcription give a sense of the paralinguistic aspects of the conversation: numbers in parentheses like (2) indicate silent pauses, in seconds. One or more colons like :: indicate a lengthening of the preceding sound. A word that appears between degree marks like º degree marksº indicates reduced volume. Underlining indicates stress. Falling intonation with a full vocal stop is marked by a period. Square [brackets] mark overlapping speech. In-drawn breath is marked with angle brackets <hhh> and exhaled breath without brackets hhh.

The exchange begins with the tutor reading aloud a portion of the student's paper in which the student is trying to describe her friend's appearance. Try reading it aloud.

Tutor   "Kyung Lim and I were in high school together. When I saw her in the class for the first time, she was in **country fashion**. Kyung Lim was little was little, was little bit bulky and usually had a ponytail on the right, right or left side of her head out of the fashion" Hum. (2) you might, you know, you might wanna use, uh, an article like a, was a little bit bulky?

Student   ah yeah.

T   [((unintelligible))]

S   **[but she said] this word and this word are**

T   the [word choice?]

S   [((unintelligible))] yeah.

T   okay. hum: you can maybe say: she was in: º country fashionº

(2) **so you mean that she was in, like hum, a style that was temporary, like contemporary for what was in style? like or how a lot of people in your country dress.**

S   (3) I: don't get it.

Up to this point, the tutor attempts to test a hypothesis for what the writer is trying to say, and the tutor asks if she wants to describe her friend's clothing as being typical for her country. But the student doesn't understand what the tutor is getting at, so she tries again.

T   okay, hum: **what do you: mea:n by when: you say country fashion. like, let's say: are you in country fashion, right now.**

S   myself?

T   yeah. do you believe you're, **do you think you're in your <u>own</u> country fashion?** or

S   [d] ah **my fash, fashion is ordinary.**

T   ordinary? [okay]

S   [yeah so]

T   **maybe you can say: instead of country fashion, she was in: plain clothes, she was simple,** hum

S   ah::

T   **is that what you mean by country fashion?**

At this point, they seem to be getting somewhere because the writer seems to respond positively to the suggestion that *country fashion* has something to do with plain or simple clothing. But then the writer says,

S   actually, actually, I'm, **I know meaning.** [w] [w] when I saw some, I saw some movie?

T   ah huh

S   they: **some people said geeky.**

T   **geeky?**

S   yeah

T   [okay]

S   [kind of] that ah huh

T   is that what you mean?

S   °yeah°

T   ((unintelligible))

S   [(hhh)]

T   [hum you can say:] she was in, so when you say country, **you
    wanna say geeky?**

S   hum :

Note the diligence here. Both the tutor and writer seem deter-
mined to get to the bottom of what the writer is trying to say
when she used the phrase *country fashion*. The writer recalls a
slang expression, *geeky*, from a movie, but does it make sense
to the tutor? The tutor elaborates on the meaning of *geeky* and
then a few moments later the word *strange* emerges:

T   or **other words for geeky,** there's, cause geeky refers to
    nerdy. hum refers to, maybe <u>weird</u>. was, when you saw her
    was that <u>weird</u> fashion to you? not, was it **strange?**

S   hh yeah.

T   yeah, cause when I first read country fashion, I thought you
    were meaning, she was in plain clothes. she was dressed as
    everyone else dresses. But if you mean <u>weird</u>, she you can say
    she was in (2)

S   hhh

T   <hhh> "she was <a little bit bulky> and usually" oh "she was
    in": you can say she was in **clo:thes I was not familiar with,**
    clothes I thought were **strange.** hum (2) <because if you say>
    <u>weird</u> clothes, it's, you don't know if everyone else think her
    clothes might have been **weird.** <u>you</u> do: . so you can say, I
    thought her clothes were **strange?**

S   °uh huh°

T   something like that. [d] does that help? or do: like
    [how that sounds]

S   **[so I can say] she was in strange fashion?**

T   you can, yeah, she was, you can strange fashion.

S   hhh ((writing))

In this example, an incomplete understanding, not a simple
misinterpretation, leads to a long and involved exchange. The
student is introduced to additional vocabulary and the nuances
that separate similar words. Interpretation occurs constantly.

The pauses give a palpable sense of the focus and concentration, which are essential because the problem—what the student is trying to say but doesn't have the words to express—is not easy to clarify or remedy, and by the end it is possible that the writer is not exactly sure what she wants to say about her friend's clothes. It is also possible that the tutor has saturated the writer with options, to the point at which the writer can no longer keep straight the various words' nuances, so she settles on *strange* even though she doesn't seem entirely satisfied with it. This conclusion is speculation, and we cannot know for sure. Instead, we must look at the evidence and do the best we can to learn from it.

Was this a productive discussion? And did the tutor make the right decision by pausing at *country fashion* and questioning it, or should she have left it alone? The answer to these questions hinges on whether the tutor, as a reader, misinterpreted the phrase or did not fully understand it. The key difference between a misinterpretation and an incomplete understanding is that in the former, the confusion is short lived and usually cleared up in a matter of seconds because the intended meaning is either one thing or the other, and the listener just needs to know which one. With an incomplete understanding, though, the participants recognize that something has gone wrong and a time-out is needed to address it. Incomplete understandings no doubt occur all the time in consultations, and they can be more valuable than we realize. Incomplete understandings create a motivating dissatisfaction, which then becomes an impetus to learning. It creates, actually, a negotiated interaction because, explicitly or implicitly, the speakers first have to see that there is a problem, then agree to work on it, and then figure out what to do about it.

Each of these moves can take time, patience, and focus. In the example above, the tutor and writer exchange twenty-one turns before they settle on the phrase *strange fashion.* Yet this doesn't seem to satisfy the writer either, and we could speculate about unexplored possibilities. Perhaps, as Ritter suggests, the writer was trying to say that her friend was *unfashionable,* but it's hard to know for sure because this word may be absent from both speakers' lexicons. And so we are back to the question of whether or not this was a productive session, a good way to spend the limited amount of time available. In this case, the tutor and writer begin with a topic meaningful to the writer, the clothes her friend wears, and with a phrase that is central to the topic. Together they discuss the meaning and use of at least eight unique but related words, testing them against the writer's intended meaning. At the same time, they become involved in an extended dialogue that involves many turns, questions, replies, and pauses for thinking. At one point, the writer suddenly recalls a word from a movie that might be a word she could use to describe her friend. In the end, the writer settles for yet another word, and they are both ready to move on.

These are some of the reasons this session is productive. The point in question, *country fashion*, seems important for the writer's purpose behind writing the paper, so the tutor is right to pause and ask about it. The pause turns into minutes as a negotiated interaction unfolds in which the student learns important distinctions between conceptually related words. Spending time with vocabulary items here, where they are part of the context, is more productive for the writer than looking them up in a dictionary, and the opportunity this tutoring session creates for her to learn the word *geeky*—it's priceless. In this tutoring session, the writer learns words in a live, one-to-one dialogue in which she can attach their meanings, unconsciously, to her feelings at the time, to the expressions she sees on the tutor's face, and to a host of other real-time factors. The student becomes involved in an extended conversation about her writing—a rare opportunity for almost anyone, and by the end of it all, she reaches closure and moves ahead.

Negotiated interaction is an essential means of teaching and learning, including and even especially when it occurs in response to incomplete understandings. Negotiated interaction, unlike other more passive forms of communication, multiplies the opportunities for learning and involves the learner in speaking, writing, reading, and listening. The one-to-one intimacy of negotiated interaction attaches to the learning. The forms of words, their functions, and how they are used in actual contexts emerge in a live and personal encounter. The fact that this episode of negotiated interaction does not end with the perfect word to satisfy everyone (there's no aha! moment) speaks to its authenticity. This incompleteness is also something worth noting because writing conferences often wrap up with loose ends. There is always a next step to be taken.

A somewhat similar conclusion is reached by Jane Cogie (2006) in a frequently cited study that looks at scaffolded learning in a tutoring session between an undergraduate tutor and a first-year student from Japan. The tutor's initial attempt to explain the structure of academic essays is unsuccessful until he switches to shorter, more concise statements the writer can understand. At that point, the writer generates ideas for his essay, and while the session ends on a positive note, the overall results are mixed. Afterward, for example, the tutor feels disappointed and comments, "Communication constraints prevailed." In examining the transcript of this tutoring session, Cogie notes that brief, comprehensible input from the tutor created a turning point for the writer, yet the tutor likely did not realize that his shift toward shorter and more concise utterances was responsible for this positive turn. Creating opportunities for tutors to reflect on their sessions, Cogie concludes, can help tutors learn to balance their responses to the complex demands of working with multilingual writers.

The examples above offer clues to the kinds of interactions with second-language writers that writing centers should encourage, namely those that

1. arise from an exigency—a specific question or problem the writer is dealing with and is motivated to address.

2. involve negotiation—the back and forth that starts with a word or idea and shuttles between questions, clarifications, explanations, examples, and possible solutions. This type of negotiation takes many turns, as opposed to a problem of simple misinterpretation, which usually leads quickly to the correct answer.

3. require patience—a pace slow enough that, if it were to occur between two native speakers, might seem like crawling. For some nonnative English speakers, and depending on the nature of the miscommunication, a slow pace is necessary to process the input of new information and to think of the words they want to use in order to contribute to the exchange, just as the writer did in the example above when she paused to recall the word *geeky* she had heard in a movie. It was not on the tip of her tongue as it would be for a native speaker, and allowing her time to access it proved successful and makes it more readily accessible in the future.

And one last point. Research shows that tutors who look back on their sessions can learn a lot about the knowledge and skills they need to improve. Cogie (2006) illustrates the value of tutors' reflections on working with multilingual writers, and Thonus (2004) describes in careful detail some of the differences between tutors' sessions with first- and second-language writers. When reading the transcript aloud, along with all of the indicated pauses, stresses, and so on, readers can begin to feel what it must have been like to be in the moment for this writer and her tutor. For purposes of tutor education, a transcript can be even better than a video recording of the session because tutors bring their own interpretations to it. Equally important, they start to see the value of examining negotiated interactions closely and how they too might record, transcribe, and analyze the data of their sessions.

COMPREHENSIBLE INPUT, OUTPUT

The terms and concepts that surround language acquisition are useful for facilitating the kinds of discussions members of a writing center staff ought to have with each other about working with multilingual writers (much as grammatical terms make it possible to talk about sentence construction). Learning the terminology can also make explicit the things L1 speakers take for granted, and it can help to make the scholarly research of the field more accessible when tutors are ready to delve into it.

The term *input* provides a good example of these benefits. To learn a second language, one not only must be exposed to and hear it but also able to make sense of it, and both of these are input. Hearing another language without understanding it is a kind of input that can aid in learning certain auditory discriminations, for example, but for the most part, what matters is input that makes sense. In the talk of a consultation, *comprehensible input* (Krashen 1982, 1985) is not merely what students hear tutors say but what they hear that they also comprehend. Intuition would tell us that comprehensible input is preferable to mere input, but then again, not understanding is sometimes the beginning of a valuable lesson.

Two points are worth noting here. First, memorization continues to dominate language instruction throughout much of the world. Particularly in traditional societies, it is already a basis for most people's encounters with literary and religious texts and with education in general. International students often excel at memorizing input, which can sometimes mask their comprehension gaps. Second, not all comprehensible input is collected in the same way.

If input is taken to represent whatever skills and abilities a language learner has already acquired, then there are skills and abilities that lie just beyond this threshold. The learner can cross this threshold if the conditions are right. Stephen Krashen (1982; 1985) names this the $i+1$ hypothesis, which says that learners go from i (input) to $i+1$ (new linguistic structures the student is ready to learn) as they come to understand their previously acquired input together with $i+1$. Tutors will recognize the similarity of this idea to Vygotsky's zone of proximal development and the ways in which writers are able to reach the upper limits of their zone with assistance from a more capable peer.

By focusing on the role of input, at least for the moment, tutors can become aware of the teaching or instructional potential of input. Passively listening to the radio or watching television counts as input for language learners, and some amount of it may be comprehensible, but listening to a radio is probably not as helpful as listening to real-world conversations. In other words, some types of input are superior when it comes to learning words in context and understanding the pragmatic aspects of language, which include things like appropriately making requests, expressing thanks, and refusing offers—all of which are necessary to being a successful language user. To learn new vocabulary words, reading them as they are used in a book is better than copying them randomly from a dictionary, even though both may be comprehensible. Input has received an extraordinary amount of attention in language-learning theory and research, in part because it can be controlled and the effect of one type can be compared to that of another. However, that attention has not come with many solutions to the problems associated with the wide varieties of input. With so many questions about input still unanswered (Gass 1997), opportunities abound for tutors to conduct research into the nature and effects of different kinds of input.

Tutors may find Krashen's (1985) input hypothesis intriguing because of its rather radical claim that comprehensible input is a necessary and sufficient reason to explain how a language is acquired—in other words, the notion that people will learn a language so long as there is input and they can comprehend it. It is a bold idea that shows up in different forms: to become a good writer, just read. Or, in terms of output, write often and a lot. Such all-or-nothing notions have a certain appeal, but are they borne out by evidence? Comprehensible input is not, it turns out, a necessary and sufficient explanation for language acquisition. It does not explain why some learners fall behind or avoid using the language, for example. These and other limitations of Krashen's idea led Merrill Swain (1985) to argue that learners need to be pushed to use what they are learning and to make it grammatically correct and appropriate. In other words, they must be coaxed to use the language (*pushed output*) and thereby create opportunities to learn, adjust, and "process the language more deeply—and with more mental effort" than is usually the case with input. "With output, the learner is in control. In speaking or writing, learners can 'stretch' their interlanguage to meet communicative goals," writes Swain (1985, 99), and thereby produce ever more comprehensible output. Swain named this the *output* or *comprehensible output hypothesis*.

If some types of input are more helpful than others, the same may be said of output. Writing an outline, draft, or notes are examples of output that generally promote learning in both L1 and L2 contexts. Reciting an oral drill is also output, but since the goal is usually to learn to use the language in actual settings, drills do not provide a real-world experience, so they are not as effective as speaking naturally. Telling their thoughts to someone or writing them down in a journal is generally beneficial for language learners (Swain 2000). Moreover, combining opportunities for input and output, such as observing new words in a book and then trying to use them in a blog post, is also helpful, as is taking a rough draft (output) to the writing center, hearing a tutor's response (input), writing another draft (output), and submitting it to the teacher and reading their comments (input).

The frequency of opportunities for various inputs, outputs, and interactions affects *automaticity*, or the ability to say or write something without having to think of how to go about it. Learners involved in frequent inputs, outputs, and interactions have more opportunities to practice using the language, and practice improves automaticity. Automaticity is different from the notion of fluency in L1 composition, in which fluency refers to the ability to write or speak a lot. Speakers can have automaticity even with short bursts of utterances, but to be considered fluent they must be able to use lots of words and to make them flow smoothly.

Where tutors sometimes fall short is in failing to modify their interactions with writers in ways that maximize learning. *Modified interactions* build on people's natural affinity for normal everyday interactions, but modified interactions change everyday interactions just enough to prompt learners to notice, think about, or alter something they have said. The intended effect is to learn from the modification and keep the interaction going. For example, a tutor says something the writer doesn't comprehend (input without comprehension). The tutor says it again but more clearly (modified input), and this time the writer looks at the tutor to indicate they still don't understand. The tutor rephrases the utterance (modified input) in a way they hope will be understandable, and just to make sure, they pause for confirmation (modified interaction). The writer understands (comprehensible input), smiles and nods, and the tutoring session moves on to something else. Modifying input by repeating and enunciating words is a fairly common and natural response, but it is easy to overuse. Such modification can also be perceived as condescending because it is also something adults do when speaking to children. Tutors need to employ lots of ways to modify interactions. In addition to modifying input by speaking clearly and rephrasing, tutors can modify the interaction itself by pausing (to give students time to recall), creating long wait times during exchanges, asking students if they know words, writing words or phrases down on paper, and helping students to figure them out from the context. Modified interactions between native and nonnative speakers occur often, according to Michael Long (1983), who identifies a number "interactional resources" participants use when they come together:

- They construct the boundaries of the practice. ("Okay, one more page and then I have to go to class.")
- They sequence actions. ("Let's look at another page together.")
- They have strategies for taking turns. ("Would you like to start reading aloud, or me?")
- They construct a participation framework. ("Since you have a list of questions, you could pick one and we'll start there, okay?")
- They construct a register of practice-specific lexis and syntax. ("Did your instructor explain the difference between summarizing and paraphrasing?")
- They make meaning in a way that is specific to the practice. ("We can say we 'thesitized' your paper!")

When students come to expect certain kinds of modified interactions, they begin to take advantage of them. In most conferences, opportunities to learn unfamiliar constructions, like the conditional form of a verb, for example, or how to use an unusual preposition like *amid*, arise fairly often, and when they do tutors must decide whether to seize them or keep going. It all depends, and tutors must use their good judgment, remembering that this opportunity may be the only one a writer will have to learn this particular point. In a class discussion, learners often hear particular constructions they would like to learn, but it's usually not appropriate to stop and ask for an explanation. In the context of a writing conference, though, consultants should make it easy to do so.

INTERLANGUAGE

Linguistic issues are among the most complex for tutoring second-language writers. One reason for this difficulty has to do with a phenomenon known as *interlanguage*, defined by Larry Selinker (1972) as a learner's developing second language that includes some of the characteristics of their first language, some of the second language they are in the process of learning, and some features that are a natural part of nearly all language-learning experience, like grammatical morphemes (e.g., tense and agreement markers) and omitting function words (e.g., articles and connectives). It's a complicated stage of language learning that contains a lot of in-betweenness, which explains some of the reasons that consultants see unevenness in a student's mastery of English. Since many second-language writers enrolled in first- and second-year writing courses are still developing their English proficiency, the interlanguage perspective is important for teachers and tutors because analyses of interlanguages show that learner errors are not random but systematic. They reflect the learner's understanding at that moment. (A sample analysis of interlanguage features in two written texts may be found in Lightbown and Spada [2006]).

Even as some aspects of a learner's interlanguage evolve to become more like the target language, however, some may not.

Transfer from the learner's L1 to the target language is one of the main reasons adult second-language learners retain spoken accents even as they become more proficient in other aspects of the new language. Aspects of the sound system of the native language continue to exert an influence on, or transfer to, the pronunciation of sounds in the new language even after years and decades of exposure. *Negative transfer* creates an interference or unwanted feature in the target, while *positive transfer* is desirable and speeds learning. An example of negative transfer is using Spanish word order when composing a phrase in English, like *shoes black*, while an example of positive transfer would be using Spanish's Roman alphabet, along with its capitalization features, to write in English.

Once something is learned, it tends to stick with you even if it you learned it incorrectly. Negative transfer and incorrectly learned rules may *fossilize*. Selinker (1972) explains fossilization as the "linguistic items, rules, and subsystems which speakers of a particular native language will tend to keep in their interlanguage relative to a particular target language, no matter what the age of the learner or amount of explanation or instruction he receives in the target language" (215). An L2 resident who is quite advanced in terms of the target language's vocabulary, syntax, and other features, yet who retains a heavily accented pronunciation with certain sounds, is an example of someone whose interlanguage pronunciation has fossilized. Fossilization can also occur with syntactic and grammatical aspects of the language, and this tends to be particularly noticeable to native speakers. Most adult learners experience some degree of fossilization, meaning they never quite reach the point at which they speak and write exactly as a native speaker would (ultimate attainment), but when and under what conditions fossilization occurs can vary considerably. Speakers may decide to retain some level of their accents, for example. In some cases, certain fossilizations cannot be overcome no matter how hard a speaker tries (Bongaerts 1999; Ioup et al. 1994; Selinker 1972; Valdés 1992).

Input, interlanguage, transfer, and fossilization are not terms to be used in the tutoring session; instead, they are useful concepts for helping tutors build a shared vocabulary with one another. They give tutors a set of concepts they can use to demystify, reflect upon, and discuss the differences they see in multilingual students' proficiency with English. They also provide inroads into research and theory in the field of second-language acquisition. Without knowing and being able to discuss the terms upon which language is organized, as well as understanding the idiosyncrasies involved in learning a second language, tutors cannot develop the tools and skills needed to have a truly successful one-to-one conference.

3
ACADEMIC WRITING

In an empirical study of writing across the curriculum, Chris Thaiss and Terry Myers Zawacki (2006) found that when faculty members are asked to describe their standards for academic writing, they tend to identify broad values that cut across disciplines:

1. clear evidence in writing that the writer(s) have been persistent, open-minded, and disciplined in study;

2. the dominance of reason over emotion or sensual perception;

3. an imagined reader who is coolly rational, reading for information, and intending to formulate a reasoned response. (5–7)

This research gives evidence of the value that faculty members place on the rhetoric of writing, or what writing does (engage readers, for example) in addition to what it says about a topic. Someone whose writing shows they have been "persistent, open-minded, and disciplined in study" establishes an ethos that colleges and universities value; those faculty and students who tend to stick with an area of interest over time, show their willingness to entertain other points of view, and situate themselves and their ideas in specific disciplines of study are rewarded. These values, and the discourses that reflect them, are rewarded not only in writing assignments and senior theses across the curriculum but also in the formal discourses faculty and administrators use when they publish journal articles, write accreditation reports, and submit evaluations of instructors' teaching effectiveness, for example. Every writer ought to learn that there is a much broader range of values underlying writing than these,

DOI: 10.7330/9780874219647.c003

however, and that even these don't reflect all expectations for writing at the college level. Consequently, it is important for students to request clear assignments and samples of the kinds of writing their instructors admire. For their part, tutors should always ask clients whether they have received these from their instructors, and if they have not, how they might obtain them or even create them with help from their tutors.

When it comes to writing at the college level, lexical development is one aspect of improvement that cuts across genres and styles, and it generally receives too little attention in the writing conference, for L1 as well as L2 students. Building and using a vocabulary that suits the writer's purpose for writing is often taken for granted. Thoughts are expressed in words, and the ability to convey ideas accurately and elegantly (in the sense of clear and to the point) is something tutors can help writers bring about. But first, it helps to have a rough sense of how the English lexicon is structured and how many words, on average, a person needs to manage. Learning a language requires a large receptive vocabulary of word families, or word stems and all their variants: so, *flame* yields *flaming, flammable, inflammation*, and so on. *Flame* is the stem and the other words are variants in the stem's family. So, the important question is, how many stems are needed to learn a language? The answer depends on many factors, but a key element is knowing what someone wants to use the language for. Auto mechanics, tailors, chemists, and information-technology specialists have large vocabularies related to their occupations, and they obviously need them for the work they do. But apart from these specialized uses, the question of how many words are needed, in general, to learn a language is worth asking because the answer illustrates the size of the challenge.

The number of words needed to read a newspaper is a good place to start because the vocabulary contained in newspaper articles has much in common with academic vocabulary: it tends to be relatively formal, uses lots of proper names, is arranged in paragraphs and headings, and is often embedded in complex sentence structures. Drawing upon a large database of articles from the news sections of major newspapers, I. S. P. Nation (2006) estimated how many word families (stems) are needed to read a newspaper and came up with eight thousand to nine thousand words. And while it is true that knowing every word is not necessary in order to comprehend a newspaper article, the percentage of words native speakers need in order to achieve good comprehension is a surprisingly high 98 percent, or forty-nine of every fifty words (Carver 1994; Hsueh-chao and Nation 2000). In other words, people who are not familiar with nearly all of the words probably do not have good comprehension of the text they are reading. To put this into perspective, eight thousand to nine thousand words is about the same number of words needed to comprehend classic novels like *The Great Gatsby* or *Lady Chatterley's Lover* (Nation 2006). For a movie like *Shrek* it is about seven thousand, and for a stretch of unscripted spoken language, roughly six thousand to seven thousand. The receptive vocabulary for most native English-speaking college students is around fifteen thousand, but this number varies considerably, with some estimates (Coxhead 2006) putting the number at more than twice as many. These figures serve as reference points, not uniform levels. The number of words needed to comprehend any text always depends on the individual reader or listener, the nature of the text itself, and whether or not there are additional cues. Movies offer an abundance of contextual cues compared to books, for example (Webb and Rodgers 2009a, 2009b). The large databases that vocabulary corpus studies rely on acknowledge these differences and try to control for them.

International students typically spend years studying English in their home countries, and many are lucky enough to attend English-medium schools. Despite the rigorous curriculum at many of these schools, students sometimes still don't learn enough English to thrive when they go abroad to college in a country where English dominates. Most international students do not enter college with the vocabulary they need for studying at the college level. (The same is true for most NES American students.) As they take classes, they must learn new words and genres and be able to use them in ways unfamiliar to them. Lee Jin Choi, a graduate tutor at the University of Illinois, observed that specific disciplines use many of the same expressions, and she pointed to a list she keeps of words and phrases so she can use them in her writing. She gave the example of *chronotopical representation* as a term that keeps coming up as she studies for her preliminary exams. She recommends keeping lists to the writing groups she leads, including lists of the mistakes they commonly make. Many writing centers are focused on helping students to learn academic written English—vocabulary as well as discourse conventions—so they can do well in the courses they are taking.

The Centre for Academic Writing at Coventry University in Coventry, England, is an example. Coventry is a college town with a diverse population of students, many of whom make their way to the center. In its statement of goals for teaching, consultancy, and research, the center uses the word *academic* eight times. According to its website, the CAW seeks to

- provide students with individualised advice and guidance on assignment writing and academic writing genres such as essays, reports, dissertations, theses and exam papers. Student support is focused on topics ranging from how to organize an academic argument to how to improve academic style and sentence structure;
- offer teaching staff guidance on designing assignment briefs, incorporating writing activities in their seminar work and on teaching writing within subject courses;
- offer research students and staff one-to-one advice on writing for publication, writing in grant proposals and other types of academic/academic-related writing.

The university's writing center is also committed to conducting research into academic writing by

- contributing to current debates in the interdisciplinary field of academic writing;
- making connections between the theories and practices of academic writing;
- informing and developing the pedagogies of academic writing (Center for Academic Writing 2004)

Vocabulary is so important that it is often taken for granted. Mina Shaughnessy (1977) acknowledges as much in her chapter on vocabulary development in one of the field's first scholarly books on L1 composition, *Errors and Expectations*, and it probably goes without saying that helping students learn to use new words is one of the goals at the Coventry center. Learning new words is easiest when we are young and not in college, where the flood of new terms can be overwhelming. Shaughnessy argues that teachers and curriculum designers must bear greater responsibility for helping students identify and prioritize key terms because there are too many to expect anyone to learn them all. The best forms of vocabulary instruction, she writes, begin with the instructor's own use of language and attentiveness to students' use of words. Her advice applies to tutoring as well.

> The teacher as mediator between the language students bring to class and the language of the academy must himself serve the students both as translator and model, trying not to lean so far toward the students' language as to misrepresent the tasks of the academy and appear foolishly adaptive, nor yet to appear so bound by the academic conventions as to be insensitive to the difficulties they pose for others. (Shaughnessy 1977, 225)

For a tutor to serve as both translator and model, it helps to keep the size of the problem of learning vocabulary in a new language in perspective. While many thousands of words may be needed to comprehend a newspaper, novel, or film, there are only about two thousand words (like *give, agree, matter*) that make up 85 percent or more of spoken and written texts regardless of subject matter (Nation and Newton 1997). For academic texts, add to these another eight hundred academic words (like *comply, evident, retrospect*) to cover an additional 10 percent, and you have 95 percent of all the words needed to cover most academic texts. Put another way, while the number of words in the English language is huge (the twenty-volume *Oxford English Dictionary* lists 171,476 in current use, over half of which are nouns), the number that most people need at any given time is manageable—about three thousand. It's the low-frequency words (*shale, kludge, petrichor*) plus field-specific technical words that present a big challenge because they number well over one hundred thousand, make up the remaining 5 percent, and are usually crucial for understanding the meaning of the discourses they are used in (Nation and Newton 1997, 239; see also Nation 2001). Again, these figures are generalizations based on analyses of large databases; your experience may vary. But while the number of low-frequency and technical words is relatively small but still significant, many technical words (at least) are defined in text or otherwise accessible in a glossary or reference book.

So, how can tutors help? One of the foremost experts on teaching and learning vocabulary, Paul Nation, offers a number of research-based suggestions, and one of these is something tutors already do: face-to-face interaction (Nation and Newton 1997, 244–48). The explanations Nation offers for the benefits of face-to-face interaction for vocabulary learning point to areas tutors can practice and reflect on:

- adjusting the level of communication to the individual student;
- developing a meaningful context;
- repeating the new terms;
- encouraging writers to use the new terms;
- allowing errors without embarrassment.

PREPARING TO PUBLISH IN ENGLISH

One of the reasons many writing centers emphasize academic writing is the growing demand for bachelor's- and graduate-level education in much of the world, especially in terms of the expansion of applied fields into academia. Nursing, for example, has traditionally been based on an associate's or baccalaureate degree plus on-site training, and while these are still the mainstay, master's and doctoral programs in nursing are widely projected to experience growing demand for the foreseeable future. Education, mental health, information science, audiology, and engineering are other examples of high-growth careers with corresponding advanced degrees.

Another key reason for the emphasis on academic writing is the dominance of English-medium publications, even in countries where English is not considered the dominant language. Two-thirds of the world's approximately sixty-nine thousand scholarly journals are published in English, according to Kenneth Hyland (2009), and the competition among authors to win acceptance in these journals is keen. An academic research study is not considered complete until it appears in a disciplinary journal, whose processes of editorial review and publication legitimize the research and confer status and reward to the author. Because of the pressure to publish in English-language journals specifically, faculty in disciplines around the world feel obligated to begin preparing students, while they are in college, to write and publish in English.

Canagarajah (2002) offers a thoughtful critique of the trend toward the growing dominance of English-medium journals in western-hemisphere countries and certain other places. Against the hegemony of this strong "center," he observes, those who live in English-peripheral regions like Africa and Southeast Asia are often shut out of the benefits of producing and consuming published research. Environmental, social, medical, and scientific problems that affect these countries in specific ways may go unstudied and unfunded unless they coincide with the interests of the western-dominated editorial boards that accept and reject articles for publication. (These interests often coincide with those of multinational agricultural, pharmaceutical, and finance industries and with the grant-funding priorities of the World Bank.) Canagarajah points to a myriad of relatively minor obstacles all writers can identify with: onerous policies for the preparation and submission of manuscripts, such as documentation styles that vary from one journal to the next, vague and confusing feedback from editors, and paying for publication.

Writing centers are not obligated to help students find ways to pay for submitting papers to their professors, but many other problems are familiar to tutors and writers, and sometimes they are felt just as intensely when conflicting standards, documentation styles, and formatting requirements among courses a student is taking overwhelm their attention. A multilingual freshman and graphic design major, Amanda Choi, said, "Teachers will say, 'You need more description,' but how much do they want? I wrote four pages of descriptive writing. In my first writing course, we had to write short sentences, and that confused me because I know writing is not all short sentences." Comments that create confusion are one thing, but sometimes they do even worse. It is not unusual for multilingual writers to receive searing comments from instructors: *this is NOT an ESL class*; *learn to use Standard English*; *you need to go to the writing center every day*; and *see me about dropping this class*. These are not respectful comments to put on any student's paper, much less those who have dedicated a significant part of their lives to learning to speak and write in English.

Fortunately, the Internet has helped young scholars collaborate and publish their work, just as it has helped students in most schools. Writing centers can also help by supporting multilingual writers and speakers as they find their way through arbitrary conventions and harsh criticisms. Sometimes tutors can refer students for help with formatting problems created by the different versions of software sold in other countries, but more often tutors are called upon to assist with language and rhetorical issues. Most schools outside the United States and Canada do not have writing curricula that lay the groundwork for academic writing, either in English or the official language. Curricula in many universities around the world are changing, and as students learn greater rhetorical awareness about writing, writing centers will play a role in helping to prepare scholars in periphery countries to "negotiate the competing discourses from the indigenous and center communities more effectively" (Canagarajah 2002, 286).

WRITING AND ACADEMIC DISCIPLINES

The European Association of Teachers of Academic Writing is an organization that explicitly promotes rhetorical self-awareness, and its focus is not limited to writing in English. EATAW brings together teachers and researchers dedicated to exploring the nature of academic writing and effective pedagogies for helping students become proficient with it. As students in expanding economies pursue higher education, advanced academic literacy provides critical links between learners and their subjects, graduate disciplines, and careers. Writing curricula at the college level are positioned across the spectrum, from broadly academic to narrowly technical; some are geared for a wide audience and some for narrow disciplinary ones. Writing tutors must work with multilingual writers to help them develop rhetorical self-awareness by recognizing these different positions even at times when they are disguised, such as an idiosyncratic requirement framed broadly, or a broad requirement applied idiosyncratically.

For ESL teachers, the distinction between "broad" and "narrow" has long been a matter of the specificity one needs to speak, write, read, and listen in certain contexts, with English for General Academic Purposes (EGAP) addressing the conventions, activities, and skills that obtain across disciplines and English for Specific Academic Purposes (ESAP) referring to the conventions, activities, and skills specific to a discipline. There is debate about these emphases because some ESL writing teachers believe students are better off when they learn general approaches to academic writing first, before they delve into the specialized norms of their disciplines (see Dudley-Evans and St John 1998; Hutchison and Waters 1987; Master 2005). Others believe students should begin learning the norms of their disciplines early on (Hyland 2004, 2009; Swales 2001).

When Thaiss and Zawacki (2006) examined the values disciplinary gatekeepers project when they talk about writing in their disciplines, they concluded that when faculty members define, enact, and evaluate writing, their values tend to vary so much that they give mixed messages to students. This occurs when professors ignore or don't recognize differences between levels of academic context: the broadly academic, the disciplinary, the subdisciplinary, the local or institutional, and the idiosyncratic or personal. "How can we teachers expect students to share our complicated expectations for writing, when we have not articulated them ourselves?" Thaiss and Zawacki ask (138–39). As students move into their majors, the standards become more specific, and some students make the transition more successfully than others. To assist all students, directors can help tutors learn to think aloud the expectations they perceive when they read between the lines of an assignment. They can also discuss with tutors the importance of professionalization, or the extent to which a student identifies with the standards and activities of their field of study and experiences success with it. For example, Ilona Leki (2007) found that one of her participants, a Japanese woman in the United States majoring in social work, came to regard writing as a process of professionalization, but not before she was able to discern the purpose of writing assignments and the key to doing well on them. She then saw that the purpose and evaluation of her work depended on simultaneously following the instructor's directions and taking ownership of her work. In other words, part of her process of professionalization was understanding her own agency in a demanding world. Another participant in Leki's study, a nursing major, saw nearly all of the writing she had to do as a waste of time, despite the heavy emphasis on writing in the nursing curriculum. She was unable to connect writing to a sense of professional identity.

In a study of L1 writing at Harvard University, Nancy Sommers and Laura Saltz (2004) found that one characteristic of successful writers is that they discover something they care about deeply; they then use writing to pursue this passion in their chosen disciplines. An engineering major might be fascinated with an alternative energy source, for example, or a health science major might be keenly interested in a disease that they feel a personal connection to. These students gain not only a personal connection to their topics and majors but significant growth in their writing skills. As they become invested in their areas of study, they plunge into reading and research, write copious notes, study hard, and often for the first time in their college careers become motivated to connect with an audience. Sommers and Saltz concluded:

> [The fact] that the students produced more self-focused arguments in their first years of college and more subject-focused arguments later is certainly true. We saw in their writing definite if not steady progression into academic discourse in all its formal aspects, including specialized diction, organization, and subject/audience relationships. That is, we saw a coincidence, perhaps a correlation, between their increased production of conspicuously public pieces and their increased ability to use the specialized language of a field (say, psychology or cultural studies) as well as their increased comfort working with its theoretical concepts and professional texts. (Sommers and Saltz 2004, 146)

Whether at Coventry University in the United Kingdom or Harvard in the United States, students of all language backgrounds need help engaging with academic discourse, both broadly and for their specific disciplines. It may be difficult for writers and tutors to always distinguish the broad conventions of academic discourse from the specific ones of an unfamiliar discipline, but the distinction is one that tutors must be aware of in order to help multilingual writers recognize the expectations they are being asked to meet, even if the writers choose to ignore or resist them. While they may not be familiar with the discourse of a writer's discipline, tutors can help writers engage with the content they are writing about by being interested readers: How did the students choose their topics? What do they find most interesting about them, and what do they like to write about? Is there a backstory to their interest in the topics? All writers, but especially multilingual writers who also struggle with language issues, can benefit from readers who appreciate their work and help them to see something in it they did not realize was there. And yet being interested and dedicated readers is by itself probably not enough to help writers succeed when they are unable to analyze or pull apart the various kinds of problems they are experiencing. For this, writers need feedback and guidance. The same is true for instructors.

A FACULTY WORKSHOP

It is one o'clock on a Friday afternoon in February in a class-room on the University of Illinois campus in Urbana-Champaign. About twenty instructors—professors, adjuncts, teaching assistants—from various disciplines have gathered for a workshop to learn about ESL students' writing. After a round of introductions, it begins with a five-minute freewrite: (1) Who are the students you are working with that brought you to this workshop? (2) What issues are you interested in exploring?

The participants share some of their responses, and then Yu-kyung Kang (Yuki), a graduate student, introduces the variety of labels used to refer to L2 students: *ESL, ELL, International,* and so forth. She observes that *L2 students* is the label used by second-language scholars as an inclusive term. In other words, it's safe to call them L2 students. Anticipating that some participants might be reluctant to say anything at all for fear of using the wrong labels, Yuki outfits her audience with terms they may not be familiar with but hopefully will start to use. In this case, what seems like a logical way to get the ball rolling is also something more. It is an offer to engage in a transaction: in return for their continued attention and cooperation, Yuki offers information and expert advice. To bolster the offer and her own credibility (above and beyond her own personal history as a multilingual working on a PhD in English), she cites a book by applied linguist Dana Ferris (2009) that discusses the many labels used to refer to L2 students.

It is hard not to notice that in the space of only fifteen minutes, many of the rituals of academic writing multilingual writers are expected to learn are also being enacted among these teachers, especially the idea that academic discourse involves interactions between speaking and writing. Some of the moves occurring in this workshop include

- outlining, or previewing the segments of the entire workshop at the beginning;
- explaining the purpose and significance, or stating the reasons the workshop is important;

- stating the goal, or telling participants what ideas they will take away from the workshop;
- positioning, or telling who the leaders are and what background and experience they have;
- involvement, or engaging the audience in Q&A, writing, discussing, or some other activity;
- anticipating the participants' concerns or states of mind;
- responding to questions and acknowledging other points of view;
- enhancing credibility by citing sources;
- defining key terms.

Qualities like these often make the difference between an interesting and engaging workshop and a dull one. They are bridge builders between the presenters and the audience. They operate in writing, too. For example, expectations for previewing, involvement, and enhancing credibility are present across most genres and circumstances, and instructors design writing assignments intended to bring out these qualities in students' writing. Unfortunately, often instructors don't make the evaluation criteria clear and often students don't see the point of the assignment anyway. Perhaps to compensate for previous failures by creating foolproof writing assignments, some instructors overdesign writing assignments and create new problems by giving students lots of hoops to jump through. These assignment writers need feedback, too.

Static rules are confusing to students because it often seems that every teacher has their own set. In a finding that will come as no surprise to students or tutors, Thaiss and Zawacki (2006) discovered that instructors assume their rules are more widely shared among their colleagues than they really are, especially the handful of specific rules they feel strongest about. Examples of rules that adherents tend to be passionate about, yet which vary widely from one instructor to the next, are the use of first person, passive voice, and contractions. Students who face high-stakes standardized tests know the consequences of rigid rules and are often at a loss for where to even find the rules. One tutor, Christopher Minaya (Bronx Community

College), explained it this way: "Teachers are teaching a million different formulas. This confuses students. Teachers say 'this is the way,' and students fail because they don't get the 'perfect' one way." Just as daunting for many students are hard-to-understand cultural references mixed with difficult words. Joanne DeCosse, a French-English bilingual tutor at the University of Manitoba, recalled a student who was overwhelmed by an assignment that made references to Scottish philosopher Adam Smith, the development of capitalism, and the word *paradigm.* "Some students just melt down, and you can tell that they're exhausted, dejected. They will seek clarification but are frustrated because they get so little return from it. They'll ask their professor, then classmates, and it escalates. But they try to be responsible," she said.

I asked Jose Luis Reyes, also a tutor at Bronx Community College, about rules. He recalled times when students brought in assignment sheets that seemed to undermine the instructor's purpose and goals by telling students to format their papers in ways that ended up consuming lots of time but hardly seemed worth it. For example, instructors who insist that their students adhere strictly to the APA stylebook probably don't realize how much time students (and the tutors who help them) devote to trying to create formats and components the stylebook calls for, like running heads, title pages formatted just so, and concise abstracts—all for a three-page paper. Another example is insisting that students adhere to idiosyncratic style sheets built around the instructor's pet peeves. Echoing remarks I heard from other tutors, Reyes said, "They get caught up in these tiny little details, and I tell them, 'Wait, you don't have to worry about that. It's not important.' I want them to work on the things that are important." Tutors bear witness to students who spend hours tracking down insignificant documentation conventions and agonizing over other details, some relevant and some pointless. Instead of creating scaffolding by which students can steadily achieve greater control and a sense of accomplishment, some writing assignments leave writers with little room to maneuver around their topics and little feeling of ownership of the final product. As one undergraduate writer, Natalia Parra-Barrero, said, "There are formats [for writing assignments] in most classes. It's not welcoming. It's not helpful. It's just the way they want it."

It's just the way they want it. The conventions of academic discourse may be seen in the context of presenting a faculty workshop or following an instructor's writing assignment. Both illuminate the performance aspect of writing, in which the performance is something observed, imitated, and audience directed, and in which students are expected to act in predictable yet novel ways. With experience, second-language speakers and writers learn to perform writing for their own purposes and to serve their own goals. Tutors who are aware of the performance aspects of writing can help writers to objectify these parts of multilingual writers' work and mitigate the aura of a "moral failing." They can help writers to notice and imitate conventions so they can use the tools of writing to achieve more important goals, like advancing in their fields of study, graduation, and a job. Ken Hyland writes:

> Academic discourse is, therefore, not only central to the ways knowledge is agreed upon and disseminated, but to what this knowledge is, how it is changed, and how it is recognized in the outside world. The idea that facts are rhetorically constructed by social communities is now no longer controversial, and research has moved to understanding how individuals use discourses to create, sustain, and change these communities. (Hyland 2009, 14)

From freshmen to full professors, members of the academic community learn to construct themselves as writers and their readers as audience, a process that relies heavily on enculturation and experience with conventions they must acquire and then prove they can use. Tutors can help writers to understand that these conventions must be learned, and they can point out conventions to imitate, especially those that function at levels beyond the sentence, like announcing the plan of their paper and defining key terms. They can also help them to prioritize major and minor conventions. A useful source for tutors to consult as they explore these ways to assist writers may be found in Teresa Thonney (2011).

METATEXT

Metatext is another type of convention and refers to the way writers convey signals to readers, usually in order to direct the readers' attention to something or to make a comment outside the immediate frame of the text. Metatext is relevant for tutors who work with multilingual writers, for at least a few reasons. Besides helping to move a session beyond discussions of grammar and mechanics, it ties the writing back to its discipline and writers to their audience. Concepts like thesis, summary, counterargument, and parallel structure are already embedded in the vocabulary of metatext because these terms give names to features of writing that can often be isolated from the rest of the text and dealt with separately in a tutoring session. Although these four terms are important, tutors need a repertoire of concepts for metatext that runs wider and deeper.

One place to expand tutors' reach with metatext is with *code glosses*, or the markers that provide additional information to readers by helping writers convey their intended meaning through rephrasing, explaining, or elaborating on something that has just been said (Hyland 2004, 2005). *Reformulation* and *exemplification* (Hyland 2007) (defined below) are examples of code glosses that seem to appear in the discourse of some disciplines more than others, and for this reason, using them appropriately is a way for writers to identify themselves as members of their chosen academic communities. Naturally, writing in one's discipline cannot be reduced to using a set of stock phrases, but corpus research has provided rather precise ways of measuring correlations between the frequency of specific discourse markers and academic disciplines, or if not the entire discipline, then at least a subset of representative journal articles.

Reformulations, exemplifications, and other code glosses create a significant difference in the quality of texts where they appear, not by themselves but cumulatively and in tandem with other features. Taken together, they can make readers feel the difference between a piece of writing that seems vague and nondescript and one that feels lucid, smooth, and generally closer to the level of writing readers expect. This is the feeling that some of the multilingual writers I interviewed told me they wanted to achieve in their writing, particularly those who had advanced literacy in their L1 and wanted to gain that same sophistication in English. Hung (Harry) D. Pham, a first-year biology major, had been in the United States for one year when I met him in 2012, but he has early memories of writing in Vietnamese. He said, "Tutors help me to use what I read in my writing because it sounds better for the reader." It is significant that Harry's notion of sounding better aligns with what he reads and achieving that same quality and style. He understands that reading in a discipline is key to writing in one, and that "sounds better" doesn't mean adorning his writing with superficialities but coming across to his readers as a knowledgeable person who expresses thoughts clearly and cogently.

Reformulations and exemplifications help to achieve such clarity and cogency. Reformulations can begin with words and phrases like *or, that is, in other words, meaning, to put it another way,* or *this is to say that.* The most common reformulation markers, in terms of sheer frequency, are parentheses, *in particular,* and *i.e.* (Hyland 2007). By way of contrast, speakers tend to say, *I mean, what I mean is, again I'll say,* or *here's what I'm trying to say.* Writers use reformulations to provide explanations or implications that help to expand or restrict the sense in which they want the reader to understand the statement that precedes the reformulations. Exemplifications can serve some of the same functions as reformulations, but as the name suggests, they signal that the writer is about to give an example. They most often begin with *such as, for example, for instance,* and *e.g.* (Hyland 2007).

Directors can help tutors become more than superficially acquainted with discoursal resources like metatext markers. First, tutors should know that when writers need to clarify a term or concept, or otherwise direct the reader's attention, it may not be wise to urge writers to add details or examples—the all-purpose vitamin of tutor advice—because these do not necessarily nail down the meaning of the concept. Instead, a reformulation of the concept may be called for in order to define it. Second, tutors should be aware that writers are more likely to use metatext markers if they are aware of them and if tutors support their appropriate use by pointing them out in published writing. And finally, it helps to know that these markers are used in a variety of ways by experienced expository writers to engage readers, and tutors who read widely will encounter them. Tutors who come to their jobs with narrow views about writing based on the belletristic conventions of literary works or who overgeneralize the conventions for writing in any discipline will almost certainly mislead the writers they tutor.

When researchers study the number of times reformulations and exemplifications occur in published journal articles, they find they are distributed unevenly instead of randomly. By scanning hundreds of published articles in eight disciplines, Hyland's (2007) corpus research shows that exemplification tends to prevail in humanities and social science fields while to a lesser extent reformulation occurs more often in science and engineering fields. This pattern of distribution is not mutually exclusive but one of tendencies. Hyland explains:

> Essentially, the sciences and engineering on one side and social sciences and humanities on the other draw on different linguistic resources in the creation of specialised knowledge. While this claim is perhaps unsurprising, it is nevertheless worth making. This is because corpus findings help to explain rather than to merely confirm our intuitions about disciplinary practices, underlining that writers' rhetorical decisions are informed by the interactions of members of communities engaged in a common pursuit. (Hyland 2007, 284)

In other words, these tendencies reflect something of the meaning making of those who create knowledge in their disciplines and thus have implications for epistemic beliefs. Hyland again says:

> Unlike scientific knowledge, which tends to be cumulative and tightly structured, researchers in the humanities and social

> sciences cannot assume that the background to a problem, appropriate methods for its investigation, and criteria for establishing resulting claims are agreed by all readers. Instead, the context often has to be elaborated anew, its more diverse components reconstructed for a potentially less cohesive readership (Hyland 2000). Exemplification plays a role here by helping to index a known and recoverable reality, keeping the relation between things in the world and discussion of those things as clear as possible. In other words, examples in soft knowledge fields represent a heavier rhetorical investment in contextualisation, perhaps even a need to persuade the reader that the phenomenon actually exists. Examples are a key means by which writers engage with their readers in this way, encouraging them to recognise phenomenon through recoverable experiences and to become involved in the unfolding text. (Hyland 2007, 272)

For any tutors or writers seeking greater knowledge of their chosen fields, it is important to know how knowledge is made and sanctioned through its spoken and written discourse. While this discussion is better left to advanced undergraduates and graduate tutors, it nonetheless belongs in the knowledge domain of tutoring writing.

Research in the field of English for (Specific) Academic Purposes yields insights about the features of texts that are considered indicators of good writing and that many writers aspire to. This is knowledge tutors can take advantage of, not so they will share this information with every writer they assist, but to expand and deepen the background knowledge of writing they can draw upon when they need it and the opportunity arises. Code glosses link abstract notions like *writing for the discipline, sense of audience,* and *explains clearly* to discoursal features that directors can teach their tutors.

LEXICAL DENSITY

Those who educate tutors should also encourage them to look closely at strings of words that make writing hard to read, not because they are technical or the subject matter is complex but because they are dense. Formidable combinations of *lexical density, nominalizations,* and *depersonalizations* (like the words that begin this sentence, in fact) occur more frequently in graduate-level writing than undergraduate writing. Readers differ in how much they tolerate them. Regardless, such constructions can obscure meaning if they are handled improperly or overused, and identifying them is the first step in helping writers to clarify their intended meaning for themselves and their readers.

More than twenty years ago, M. A. K. Halliday and Ruqayia Hasan (1989) pointed out that lexical density is cognitively taxing and slows reading because it elevates the number of content words relative to the number of function words like articles, prepositions, and conjunctions, making sentences short, compact, and less explicit. They show the contrast with this example:

> *Investment in a rail facility implies a long-term commitment.* vs. *If you invest in a rail facility this implies that you are going to be committed for a long term.* (61)

Sentences like the first are common in academic writing, and those like the second less so. Heavily nominalized and depersonalized phrases grow more daunting when they hook up with passive (and passive-like) constructions that deemphasize actors in favor of third-person points of view and metaphorical subjects, phrases like "the evidence demonstrates" or "as Appendix A shows." The example below contrasts a relatively dense, nominalized, and depersonalized construction with one that is not.

> *Adherence to a rigid ideology requires a vigorous defense.* vs. *Critics require anyone who adheres to a rigid ideology to keep up a vigorous defense.*

The second sentence is longer and some would argue wordier. It also arguably changes the meaning by specifying an agent, critics. It is worth tutors' time to ponder the subtle yet cumulatively significant differences between alternate forms such as these. Expressing actions with nouns instead of verbs, as the nominalizations do in the first sentence, is somewhat like slowing down a movie and examining it frame by frame, freezing the action so it can be commented upon. (Nominative absolute constructions are often used for this purpose in poetry and fiction: *The ship's captain stumbled into the darkness,* <u>hands outstretched and reaching for the guide rail</u>.) Using nominalizations can be useful when focusing on images or concepts one at a time is necessary, but when this is not the goal, then strings of sentences that accumulate paragraph after paragraph in this way slow readers to a crawl. Though they may be grammatically well formed, nominalizations can add to the difficulty of reading a second-language writer's accented text.

Directors can take at least two points from this. One is that tutors must be able to read such texts in order to understand what the writer is trying to say. Then they must be able to discuss these texts with the writer in a negotiated manner. In other words, tutors must approach the text tentatively because the writer's intended meaning may not yet be fully developed, or it may be developed but not well formed. In either case, the starting point must be a discussion of the writer's intended meaning that does not presume too much about what they are trying to say. The other point is that tutors must be able to identify, once the meaning is clear, the readability problems that arise when readers feel overwhelmed by a confluence of obstacles such as dense lexical constructions plus missing words plus minor errors and so on. It is challenging, in a tutoring session, to address these problems while also not eliminating the multilingual writer's accent when the writer wants to maintain it. It can be hard for tutors to chart a course for accomplishing this, but one way is to raise writers' awareness for distinguishing between errors they make naturally and unavoidably (in the use of articles and prepositions, for example) and the rhetorical choices they can control. Tutors can alert writers to their capacity for writing clear, readable prose by reducing nominalizations and agentless passives while sustaining the accented forms that emerge in the use or omission of articles and prepositions.

VOCABULARY

Learning vocabulary in a new language, along with learning to become comfortable using it, are critical for language learners (Coxhead 2006). As language learners encounter new words through reading, listening, and perhaps exercises, they then must try the words out before they can become part of their active vocabulary. Tutors can be a good audience to practice on. Using a just-learned new word is not for the fainthearted, as anyone who has ever tried it and been laughed at will attest. In the faculty workshop at UIUC we saw earlier, Yuki does not take for granted her audience's comfort level with discussing multilingual writers. She defines terms like *L2* and *ELL* and reassures them that it is okay to refer to them as L2 students. Using an accurate, varied, and appropriate vocabulary is something all language learners strive for, but doing so poses a big challenge for multilingual writers. As tutors become involved in helping multilingual students with vocabulary, directors can remind the tutors of the critical role vocabulary plays in language learning and of the need to encourage writers to take risks and use new words in order to fully retain them.

Sarah Nakamaru (2010) has conducted one of the few studies of vocabulary in writing center tutorials involving international students. She found that tutors were able to focus on the students' lexical needs, but afterward, when the tutors were asked to describe what occurred in the session, there was a problem. According to Nakamaru, "The tutors characterized the feedback they provided in the session in terms of 'content' and 'grammar,' almost completely failing to articulate the lexical needs of the students" (110). Nakamaru suggests reasons the tutors lapsed into the familiar *content* and *grammar* when characterizing the sessions, including the fact that these terms have become so commonplace that it is hard for tutors to think otherwise. Perhaps tutors see students' writing and the work of tutoring as a bifurcated world of content and grammar.

As we saw earlier, many thousands of words must be learned to read even a daily newspaper, and college-level reading requires many more still. Ilona Leki (2007) describes a fairly common set of difficulties for students in majors like nursing that involve more than one discourse and have both technical and professional vocabularies. In the medical field, examples include the names of diseases, medicines, and human body parts, as well as a plethora of abbreviations (81–82). To establish a good rapport with their patients, nursing students also must use common, everyday language. For one of the students in Leki's study, Yang, this meant she had to learn double the number of vocabulary words as her native English speaking counterparts did. Even as she acquired new technical and common words rapidly, Yang still had occasional difficulty with simple ones, like the comment "well done" that a professor had written on her paper. When asked about it, Yang said she thought the professor meant that she had done enough. When Leki pressed her further in the interview, it turned out that Yang thought a well-done paper was like cooked food—both are done enough. Misunderstandings like these are not unusual even for advanced learners. Yang had been in an English-speaking country for nine years and had attended an English-medium university for several of these, but common words and expressions still sometimes eluded her, not because she wasn't a good learner but because there are so many and learning them takes time and practice.

The process of learning vocabulary is not simply additive, and an individual's productive and receptive domains of language acquisition don't necessarily match up. A writer may have difficulty coming up with the words for composing an essay (production) but relatively little trouble reading and understanding an advanced-level textbook (reception). A tutor reading the writer's work may underestimate the number of words the student knows, when actually the writer needs to make greater use of the words already in their receptive vocabulary and could benefit from a tutor who helped them to do this. For some individuals, production and reception may diverge considerably, and different types of production or reception may differ too. These differences can cause problems for some students when, for instance, their speaking vocabulary appears limited compared to their writing vocabulary. Some readers may doubt that the writing is the students' own work. The difference, however, may be the result of many factors, including normal stylistic variation, the use of a dictionary and thesaurus, or the input from a tutor. All of these factors play a part in providing students with the tools they need to achieve success in their writing.

TRANSLATION

Students bring drafts to the writing center that are the products of translation more often than we probably realize. One way students translate is to write the first draft of their papers in their L1 and then translate this draft into English with the help of a dictionary and perhaps a peer. Francesca Salomon, a first-year legal studies major in 2012 who was born in Haiti and came to the United States in 2010, said, "When I write, I think of it first in Spanish and then I translate it into English. That's what I do. It's not really complicated." Amionne Jean, a writing fellow at Nova Southeastern and an English-Creole bilingual born in Haiti, would say it *is* complicated. Amionne enjoys working with other multilingual students in part because she understands the impulse some learners have to translate and she tries to help them by warning against it. She explained:

> Being bilingual has definitely played a role in understanding the students I've tutored, especially those who speak English as a second language. Some of the students that I've worked with in the past know that I am bilingual, and most of the students that I am working with now also know this. Even though I've never had a problem writing in English, I can see how difficult it can be to think in another language and attempt to translate those thoughts in English. There are certain expressions in Creole that cannot be directly translated in English, so I imagine that ESL students who try to do the same will eventually run into many problems.
>
> Even though the ESL students that I've worked with thus far did not speak Creole, I find that I can still relate to them. So I find that being bilingual helps me to be understanding and patient with ESL students who struggle in their composition courses. So far, ESL students seem to be the ones that regularly schedule sessions with me. Last semester, one ESL student scheduled ten sessions (out of the recommended three) with me, and this semester, one ESL student has met with me twice for one assignment (the recommended amount is one). I wouldn't rush to assume that this is because I'm bilingual but I find it interesting to note that I seem to have a better time tutoring someone who is bilingual than someone who is monolingual.

Translation practices in second-language writing are controversial. Years ago experts believed that translation interfered with fluency and audience awareness in second-language writing, but today they tend to have a more nuanced view of it. Janet Bean et al. (2011) offer such a perspective, noting that, as part of the second-language writing process, translating can delay learning when students come to depend on it. Translation has benefits, though. It can serve as a bridge to writing in English when, for example, students use their L1 to get their thoughts down on paper and then use their developing knowledge of English to revise and edit. Bean et al. conclude:

> If this rewriting/revising approach proves beneficial in further research and classroom trials, it will yield a point of strategic leverage: when students compose in a language other than English and then rewrite/revise wholly in English—not seeing the lexicon and syntax of their home language and not trying to stay tied to it—they will get a double benefit: the benefit of composing or inventing in their home language, but also the benefit of *composing again in English* and thus practicing and developing a kind of syntactic fluency in the target language. This approach thus cuts through the over-simple either/or choice about whether to compose in standardized English or some other language: students can practice composing in both languages. (Bean et al. 2011, 241)

The practice of translating to compose in English, as described above, creates opportunities for both tutors and writers. A tutor who is studying the writer's L1 as a foreign language, for example, stands to learn as much from a translation-based session as the writer. Otherwise, the tutor and student can collaborate in the composing process, including discussing the nuances of meaning that separate one expression from another. This kind of interaction is valuable for learning formal and informal usages, double meanings (like "well done"), and certain items of cultural knowledge, which can be particularly opaque.

Harry Pham, a first-year writer at Nova, expressed his frustration with encountering numerous cultural references in assigned readings.

> I'd like my tutor to help me use what I read in my writing so that it sounds better. Like a metaphor, for example. I don't understand it, but I bring it to the tutor and one guy helped

me. It's very hard for international students to understand what is the, the underground? meaning of a metaphor. For example, Frederick Douglass *Slave Narrative*. There's a reference to nineteen lashes and to something in the Bible, but I have never read it [the Bible]. But the professor, he talked a lot about this and it was hard to understand.

Another kind of translation seems less beneficial. Google Translate, Translator Toolkit, and the many online networks of translators are used widely. It is important to know when a writer is relying heavily on a translator so the tutor can keep the session focused on the writer's ideas instead of being an editor who corrects translation inaccuracies. Tutors can inquire about use of a translator when there are indications of disjointed sentences and oddly misused words. Directors and multilingual tutors can help one another find ways to talk with multilingual writers about their use of translators and the limitations of using third-party translators. At the same time, it is worth considering the role that machine translators already occupy in business, technology, and government and the increasing reliance on them that is sure to grow as software programs and the massive databases they draw from become more sophisticated. What part will machine translations play in the multilingual writing centers of the future? What role will tutors have? To put it another way, what do writers want from their tutors? It is easy to get caught up in the mechanics of writing (*no comma here, indent there*) and tutoring (report forms, schedules, and please-turn-off-your-cell-phone), but often what makes the most difference to writers is what moves them.

"SHOW THEM HOW LANGUAGE CAN RAISE YOU UP"

Patrick Gourdet is blue eyed with short hair. He moves his body when he talks. Patrick's father is from Haiti and his mother is from Germany, where he was born. The family moved around a lot, and Patrick grew up a German-English bilingual. As a teen, when he didn't want his father to know what he was saying, or when he just wanted to be obstinate, he spoke German. Now, at age thirty-two, he is double majoring in computer science and math with a minor in writing. "Because we were constantly moving, I never learned writing or spelling," he told me. "I was always moving from one school, state, or country to another and there was no continuity." He recalled these years wistfully. "In writing, I would get a lower grade than I thought I deserved, but the feedback was never specific enough that I could know what I did wrong." Back in Germany after seventh grade, he ended up in the lowest track, where he remembers spending an inordinate amount of time trying to learn the rules for capitalizing nouns. He was moved to the "catch-up track" and developed an interest in graphic arts, but then his family was off again, this time to Amsterdam, then Italy and Morocco. Meanwhile, he wrote songs and poems in German and English. "German was a little easier for me," he said. "German is more descriptive, but English is easier to rhyme." He read and wrote a lot and continued to struggle with spelling.

Patrick was in his first semester in college in the United States when he was assigned to write a personal-experience essay. He wrote about a toy he received when he was around four or five years old. Playing with the gift turned out to be one of those childhood moments he has never forgotten. He and a boy were playing with it, and the only thing Patrick remembers is that, suddenly, the boy smashed it. "The essay," he recalled, "was torn to shreds. I put a lot of myself into it, but that didn't matter to the teacher." From a social-constructionist perspective, many of Patrick's difficulties might be traced to the disruptions in schooling that made it hard for him to organize knowledge like spelling rules and the resultant discontinuities in social relationships that precluded academic peer groups. Instead of being part of a community of learners, he was often on his own and always starting anew. From a critical pedagogy perspective, Patrick's story highlights ways in which schools assign disproportionate importance to form-based features of writing like spelling and capitalization over and above the creation and negotiation of meaning. Seared into his memory is the punishing act of an essay "torn to shreds." From a postmodern perspective,

Patrick lives, works, and studies among one of the most ethnically diverse populations in the United States and is someone whose rich bilingual, multiracial, and multicultural history places him at the crossroads of new and hybrid discourses.

Social constructionism, postmodernism, critical pedagogy, or others—these perspectives all provide useful models for learning, and they give tutors ways to begin to organize the range of needs and experiences writers bring to the writing center, but none of these models completely fits an individual writer. The disruptions in schooling and community made growing up a challenge for Patrick, but the disruptions also proved to be a source of opportunity and excitement. "The great thing about growing up bilingual and moving as often as I did meant I picked up languages but it also made me susceptible to everyday little challenges," he said. He learned from an early age that he would be a traveler and live in different parts of the world.

The increasing mobility of people like Patrick the world over will continue to be a fact of life for schools and communities. Students will find continuities on their own, learn to live without them, or find curricula adapted for an increasingly mobile society. The one-to-one pedagogy of writing centers can be a refuge for students who feel displaced, but these pedagogies must accommodate the ways people's lives are changing. Tutoring online is a start. Patrick could have benefitted from a portfolio of his learning and accomplishments. He would have benefited, too, from feedback on his writing that made sense in one school and still made sense in another. Along the way he gained the ability to talk about his music with sophistication, but not so much about his writing even though he was a writer. Listening to Patrick talk, you can sense that school, in general, let him down.

Critical pedagogy has transformed much of the thinking about education but tends to have its favorite targets, like the privileging of teacher knowledge, memorization, and anything that tips the balance of power away from learners. There is no excuse for mean-spirited responses like the one Patrick recalls from his first year in college, but at one point in the interview he lamented feedback that was never specific enough to help him know what he did wrong. Patrick was aware that feedback helps in learning a language, and he expected such feedback from his writing teachers. In the United States, where most schools operate under the precepts of a monolingual culture, multilingual learners sometimes struggle in classrooms where implicit teaching holds sway. As Jennifer Staben and Kathryn Dempsey Nordhaus (2009) have pointed out, nondirective or implicit tutoring keeps multilingual students at a disadvantage because it privileges cultural knowledge and birthright intuitions about English. Patrick came across to me as someone who has a well-developed critical sense of the role literacy has played in his own life and in the world, but he also made it clear that he wishes the schools he attended had been more accountable to him as a learner.

The outlines of postmodern approaches to tutoring have been poignantly drawn in the writing center literature by Nancy Grimm (1999), Anne Geller et al. (2007), and Anis Bawarshi and Stephanie Pelkowski (1999) as well as in the field of second-language studies by Alastair Pennycook (2001), Vivian Zamel (1997), and others. Zamel's transculturation model, for example, stresses the fluidity and merging of identities and discourse boundaries. While appealing in its emphasis on human agency, the model also rejects categories and seems to allow for so many possibilities it is hard to know where to find boundaries, though they exist. Maybe some models depict a world that is easier to navigate than it really is, or easier than the one Patrick grew up in.

Toward the end of my interview with him, Patrick said, "Growing up as I did taught me about being taken seriously by other people. I learned what I could do with languages and what I couldn't. This made me more aware." He paused for a few seconds and continued. "Today I see people who don't seem to care how they speak or come across, that whatever they say in English is good enough. But it's not. I know that firsthand. People will judge you on how you speak, and that's a fact. It's not just about the language, it's also how you come across—what you wear, body language, too. You have to show people respect and earn their respect of you. Nobody benefits when this doesn't happen."

"How do you think tutors should come across to students?" I asked him.

"Lead by example," he said resolutely. "Show them how language can raise you up." Long pause, eyes locked on.

Multilingual students are a diverse group of individuals who carry the cultural baggage it takes to learn what they know, even when the baggage includes learning English from teachers who may have let them down. Writing centers are supposed to be places that lighten the load, even for a while, because students expect to find tutors who not only want to help but also possess enough knowledge and understanding about writing and language that they can, when students are ready, raise them up.

The fact that writing centers are organized not with students grouped into classes but one by one makes a difference. Tutoring begins with relationship but turns on effort and achievement. One tutor who wrote me from Northwestern College in Iowa said:

Some differences [among students] are cultural. I have tutored people from across the U.S. as well as international students. I helped a girl from California who is bilingual but does not have a firm grasp on English writing. I also tutored a girl from Kenya as well as a boy from Brazil. Each of these individuals had a different struggle with English writing. Sometimes it was the expression of their ideas in English. Other times it was trying to convey a cultural aspect of their lives that Americans would not recognize. Sometimes, an American student not from the Midwest has difficulty describing something to me, a small town Midwest girl, that doesn't need explanation back home. These glimpses into other cultures are fascinating. After I have attempted to understand a concept, trying to translate it into American terms causes me to sympathize with their struggles.

This tutor refers to the hard work of trying to understand concepts and convey them across cultures as well as the feelings of sympathy this work gives rise to. When you put the words of this unlikely pair side by side —Patrick, a multiracial bilingual male of thirty-two who has lived all over the world, and the "Midwest girl" at a small college in Iowa—what comes through is a shared desire for individualized teaching and learning through the building of relationships based on mutual respect and a sense of caring.

Interview data rarely speak words that write conclusions, and interpreting this data does involve some reading between the lines. People of all blends live and work close to the ground, inhabiting a place both above and below the sweep of theory but never fully in it.

4

CORRECTIVE FEEDBACK

The idea that students write in order to be corrected by teachers has overshadowed much current writing instruction in the United States in part because it has such deep roots. When the course we know today as first-year writing (or freshman composition) started at Harvard University in the 1870s, it followed on the heels of a surge in student enrollments that brought with it a degree of ethnolinguistic diversity never before seen on campus. Documents at the time reveal some of the emotion behind deeply held biases. One Harvard professor equated good writing to "grammatical purity" free of "blunders which would disgrace a boy twelve years old" (Brereton 1995). Eliminating these errors from students' writing became such an obsession that instructors took on the role of disciplinarians in charge of large classes and required daily themes whose main purpose was to elicit writing that contained as few errors as possible in grammar, spelling, and punctuation. Today's teachers and tutors are no longer disciplinarians, though writers still want to have as few errors as possible.

ERRORS

Researchers are still interested in the causes and treatment of error in student writing but less so today for reasons of purity and punishment than for the recognition that error is a natural part of learning to speak and write. This shift came about partly as a result of an influx of ethnolinguistically diverse students in the 1960s and '70s and the publication of Mina Shaughnessy's (1977) *Errors and Expectations*, which turned the tide from

DOI: 10.7330/9780874219647.c004

thinking of errors as moral flaws to seeing them as steps along a journey toward greater writing proficiency. Since Shaughnessy, L1 writing researchers, and to a lesser extent L1 writing teachers, have believed that the best "treatment" for error is to accept that errors are part of the learning process and will diminish with age and experience. Compositionists and linguists still believe errors tend to reflect writers' literacy background, age, and experience, but not any moral failings.

Notions of error in the field of second-language acquisition make an important distinction between *error* and *mistake*, where an error is something learners say or write incorrectly and usually cannot recognize or repair on their own because they doesn't know the rule behind it, while a mistake is something they can both recognize and repair because they have learned the rule and can apply it. For this reason, tutors usually find that errors are repeated consistently and show a clear pattern. Mistakes are more random and occur equally among native and nonnative speakers. Tutors can see the distinction between errors and mistakes play out when they observe writers rereading drafts of their papers and correcting their own mistakes while skipping over errors. (Actually, writers often skip over mistakes as well because they fail to notice them; they may be reading too quickly or thinking about something else. When this happens, the problem is not one of teaching or learning rules but of *noticing* [see below], and the solution is to help writers find ways to pay closer attention to them.) Selinker's (1972) theory of "interlanguage" is relevant here because it describes an approximation of the target language that evolves as learners acquire more and more control. What tutors may see as random errors in a student's writing may be, on closer inspection, features of the interlanguage, which includes instances of overgeneralization (e.g., applying the possessive marker to pronouns, like *his's*), simplification (e.g., regularizing verb forms like *catched*), interference errors or features transferred from the learner's L1, and features of the second language.

"What is most clear, however, is that it is often difficult to determine the source of errors," say Patsy M. Lightbown and

Nina Spada (2006, 82). In the case of both first- and second-language writing, it is hard to know why writers make some errors and not others, and it's hard to know which errors are not even available for inspection because the writer has avoided them altogether. On top of these questions, there is the puzzle of which errors readers find most troubling and therefore which ones tutors and teachers should help writers to avoid. There are many contextual variables to control, like how many errors there are, what counts as an error, whether or not readers expect to find errors, whether they are bothered by them, and whether they even notice them.

Seungku Park teaches intensive English for basic and intermediate English learners, and he believes the focus on error that many multilingual writers carry with them stems from the culture of testing in which they learned English.

> ESL academic life starts when they start learning English to pass a standardized English language test, such as TOEFL and IELTS, which are the measurement for international students' academic English for North American universities and colleges. They are so accustomed to finding a correct answer when they study for the English language tests that they are likely to assume that there is a "correct writing." In addition, many international students are not aware of the difference between proofreading and revising.

Instead of developing better writers, which is ultimately most teachers' goal, cultures of testing develop test takers and proofreaders. Students become accustomed to memorizing information for a test, reading examples, and viewing corrections. When it comes time for their own writing, instead of using creativity and judgment, students focus on what they think is the correct way.

Consistent with the test culture Park describes, many schools that teach English around the world have inherited the audiolingual method of instruction. It became popular during World War II and in the years following the war as a way to train people in speaking and listening to other languages. The classic audiolingual method relies heavily on drill and practice while paying relatively little attention to context-based meanings and the pragmatic aspects of language. Though still widely used in many countries, teachers and researchers have embraced alternative approaches that use more holistic methods. Communicative language teaching (CLT) is perhaps the most popular of these methods. In a classroom that uses a communicative approach to language teaching, students are involved in conversations and problem solving across the modalities of speaking, writing, reading, and listening.

By focusing on drill, repetition, and accuracy in the use of the language, the audiolingual method and the teaching of written grammatical correctness came to be seen as outmoded and ineffective, shifting pedagogy from issues of language at the micro level to the macro. Nonetheless, microlevel concerns are still critical to producing and comprehending discourse at any level, and second-language learners experience these concerns far more acutely than native speakers. "Attention to language is often presented as editing or proofreading," writes Sarah Nakamaru (2010) "and is almost always equated with 'grammar,' despite the fact that having access to and being able to effectively use English words and phrases (i.e., lexical knowledge and skills) is crucial to creating meaningful written texts in English" (95).

Writing centers have earned a reputation for dismissing students' concerns about editing and proofreading. In 1984, in one of the first books on training writing center tutors for L1 writing, Reigstad and McAndrew (1984) drew a clear line between higher- and lower- (or later-) order concerns (HOCs/LOCs), insisting that issues of grammar, syntax, and punctuation take a back seat to higher-order concerns like content, focus, clarity, audience, and organization. They followed in the tracks of L1 compositionists, who have generally marginalized research and pedagogies that address sentence-level language concerns for the past several decades. An article in the inaugural issue (Halstead 1975) of the *Journal of Basic Writing*, for example, called upon teachers and researchers to "put error in its place" by concerning themselves only with errors that interfered with comprehensibility. In retrospect, this recommendation seems misguided at a time when research has also shown that word- and sentence-level concerns related to formal accuracy cannot be easily separated from comprehension and meaning.

Carol Severino et al. (2013) have recently looked into the HOCs and LOCs binary and have shown how they often overlap. Severino et al. are not the first to recognize the confluence, but they contribute to our understanding by drawing the concept of *error gravity* into the debate, noting that in applied linguistics, error gravity refers to a scale or continuum rather than a dichotomy or hierarchy like HOCs/LOCs. Error gravity helps explain why LOCs become HOCs by focusing on readers', listeners', and other interlocutors' experiences with incomprehensibility arising from different types of errors, the particular severity of errors, and especially their cumulative and sometimes irritating effects. These conclusions are supported by Larry Beason (2001), whose follow-up interviews with a group of nonacademic readers show that while readers have varying responses to the severity of common errors found in writing, errors do tend, on average, to harm the writer's image and credibility.

And students seem to know that they do.

Antoine Dahdah Sayegh studied English in a bilingual school in Venezuela starting at age six and came to the United States when he was eighteen. A fluent English speaker, he talked about what he looks for in a tutor: "Supporting me but telling me what to change and fix. I like critics. It makes me feel better. I know that tutor is telling me the truth, is not hiding anything from me. Tell me what's wrong with my grammar."

The contrast between what Antoine said and what another writer, Brittany Bacallao, told me, is stark. "I still remember a comment I received from one of my writing teachers," she said in a low voice. "'This doesn't make sense.' I couldn't believe it— what part of it doesn't make sense?" she wondered. It is usually the case that writers don't mind negative feedback as long as they perceive it to be constructive. If the criticism is too harsh, students react with frustration or resignation. However, if the criticism is too vague, writers do not know how to fix it.

It is common for writers to want tutors and teachers to correct their errors and to be disappointed when they don't, but this does not mean they want tutors or teachers to do nothing but correct errors. Writers regard corrective feedback as an opportunity for them to learn as they move along the road to greater accuracy, fluency, and control. Lack of confidence in their abilities is not something writers like Antoine struggle with. They do, however, struggle with a lack of constructive feedback from tutors and teachers who are not forthright and knowledgeable when writers seek their help. Researchers disagree on when and how to engage in error corrections (Bitchener and Ferris 2012), but it is clear that teachers across the disciplines are sensitive to errors and expect students to be vigilant about them (Santa 2006). Multilingual writers take this vigilance seriously and tend to expect tutors to do so. Ignoring or contravening writers' requests for feedback on their errors has opened writing centers to criticism for failing to take seriously multilingual writers' requests for help with language and grammar, and for succumbing to the monolingual bias that treats errors the same way for native speakers, who can fall back on their intuitions about what sounds correct, and nonnative speakers of English, who cannot.

Compositionists will likely always argue about error (Santa 2006), while the reality of helping students to do well on their writing assignments means that tutors must begin somewhere when error correction is the main goal. Cynthia Linville (2009) distinguishes between serious errors, which interfere with meaning, and treatable errors, which students can usually learn to identify and correct themselves because such errors are governed by rules, for the most part. She proposes six types of treatable errors: subject-verb agreement, verb tense, verb form, singular/plural constructions, word form, and sentence structure. This list may not be definitive, but it serves to illustrate the contrast between thinking about errors in the abstract versus in an actual piece of writing. Without guidance from their directors, tutors tend to take up errors with writers one at a time as they come across them in reading a draft. A better way is to analyze them according to how treatable they are. For example, errors the writer fails to notice can be addressed first. On the other hand, errors involving articles and prepositions can be very hard to treat; so long as they do not interfere with meaning (preposition errors sometimes do, article errors usually don't) can be put off until later. Similarly, treatable errors that happen to occur in convoluted syntax should wait until the meaning and sentence structure are sorted out. And so on.

Tutors need to keep in mind another important finding from research, discussed in detail by Polio (2012), and that is the commonsense but often overlooked realization that writers must attend to the feedback they receive. Put another way, corrective feedback from tutors and teachers is useless unless writers pay attention to it, keep track of their errors, and strive to overcome them. Sachs and Polio (2007) found that having students simply spend time looking at their corrected errors for fifteen minutes had a positive impact on their writing. Fortunately, tutors can play an important role here by helping writers to record their most common errors and following up with the writers on subsequent visits. Writing centers that keep good records from one visit to the next are a benefit to all students who need to track their errors.

One of the hallmarks of writing center practice is that writers and tutors set the agenda together when they discuss the priorities for the session. When the outcome of this discussion is a decision to look for errors, the next question should be about how to do so interactively. Hints and encouragement are familiar enough to tutors, and they sometimes work. As Valerie Makowiecki, a former writing center tutor who now tutors privately near Philadelphia, stated, "Sometimes I need to give hints on how to find their mistakes, but I never give them answers and the easy way out. I always encourage them to find and fix their mistakes. That's important because it's their work and they will better learn and remember if they do it on their own. Also, encouraging them to use resources goes along with learning to discover unknown things on their own." Valerie understands that if she provides both the problem and the solution, her student will not retain the knowledge necessary to avoid making that mistake again. She must prod the student to discover the problem, then give that student the clues to the solution in a way that cements the information for the future.

Valerie is a tutor who manages hints in subtle ways, but what does this approach look like exactly? Corrective feedback depends on modified conversational strategies for its effectiveness. These strategies tend to come more naturally to well-trained teachers than they do to tutors because they are unlike conversations most people are accustomed to. Outside of school, such conversations come across as pedantic and condescending. This same danger is present in the writing center because finding and correcting errors requires modifying the conversation in order to direct attention, and this modification feels, and in fact is, controlling—unless it is framed properly in advance and the writer agrees to it (for example: *Before we start, let's make a plan. When you see an error, go ahead and correct it. When I see an error, I will either pause or repeat it, okay? Does this seem like a good plan?*) These modified conversations include tutor questions like comprehension checks (*Is the example clear?*), clarification requests (*Do you recall the rule for count nouns?*), and repetitions. Effectiveness depends on paying attention to some things and ignoring almost everything else. It can be hard to do.

GETTING NOTICED

The need to focus a learner's attention led Richard Schmidt (1994) to propose *noticing* as a key element in second-language learning because unless learners are focused on what they should be learning and not on something else, it doesn't matter how good the instruction or interaction is. Noticing applies best to situations where the task is specific, like spotting certain words and phrases, and where there is ample opportunity to encourage noticing, like the one-on-one context of a tutoring session.

To make noticing part of the interaction of tutoring, tutors can begin with a brief discussion about what the writer wants to look for and then talk about what would help the writer to do that. The writer might say "read slowly" or "tell me when it's wrong." Since the idea is to get writers to notice a specific word or phrase, it is often necessary to help them spot it, and writers usually have a preference for how this is done. A tutor who points with a finger or pen might make the writer feel awkward, especially if the session is out in the open where others can see, or if the writer comes from a culture where finger pointing is considered rude. Reading aloud and pausing or raising a hand from the table might be a better way. Using the edge of a blank sheet of paper to cover up all lines except one is an old stand-by, but it is an artificial way to read and sometimes does not focus the writer's attention narrowly enough. As Schmidt points out, noticing is different from awareness in that learners may be aware of a rule but not notice that they have broken it or that it even applies in certain cases. In writing, noticing is the first step toward making a correction, adjusting awareness, and achieving better understanding.

A few years ago, I tried to think of a way to help a class of students who were preparing for a standardized writing exam to notice and understand the difference between two punctuation marks that are easily confused, colons and semicolons, which the students in this class seemed to be using interchangeably. I came up with this: "Look at the two dots in a colon. These are two open eyes and they are saying, 'Look at what's ahead of you—it is something you must pay attention to.'" (I raised my right hand and pointed two fingers to my eyes and then pointed them toward the class. We all smiled.) We looked at examples and they got it. Then we talked about semicolons. "Two eyes open? No, one is winking, and saying 'I'm really a period, disguised as a semicolon.'" We looked at more examples and they got that too.

Whether this lesson really worked or not, I can't say. I thought I noticed an improvement in their writing, but perhaps they simply avoided using colons and semicolons altogether. Maybe they found the demonstration so silly they vowed never again to use colons and semicolons. It's hard to know, in teaching and tutoring, whether you're having the effect you intend.

Sometimes, especially in face-to-face interactions, writers tend to nod in agreement even when they don't completely understand, leaving tutors with the impression that things are going better than they really are. In any case, the point of the example here is to illustrate that noticing is a cognitive function that requires some type of activation. Drama, humor, or emotion, when delivered in small doses, can be effective. Drawing something out helps make it stick, too. Noticing is all about drawing attention to the problem in a way that makes the student think cognitively about it. If done effectively, you won't just fix the problem in the paper, you'll likely permanently fix it altogether.

RECASTING

One of the most useful tools in a tutor's belt is *recasting*, a strategy that both focuses attention and suggests a correction. A recast repeats what the writer wrote without the error. For example, a student writes, "Last week I write him an e-mail," and the tutor repeats, "Last week you *wrote* him an e-mail." Recasts may or may not provide the correct answer, depending on the situation. They can be an efficient way to keep a tutoring session on track by getting students to notice a problem, correct it, and move on.

There is a problem, however, when the tutor, not the writer, becomes the one who notices, corrects, and moves on. Soha (not her real name) is a multilingual graduate student working with Morgan (not his real name), a native English-speaking consultant and also a graduate student at the campus writing center in the midwestern United States. Soha has asked for help with the grammar and structure in an art history paper. Morgan invited her to read aloud, but Soha shook her head and said "because of my pronunciation." Perhaps they both felt a bit self-conscious because of the observer seated about eight feet behind them.

The session is remarkable for its all-over-the-map quality. Morgan begins reading and stops when he has a question about focus. Soha responds, a brief discussion follows, and the tutor reads on. He spots an unclear term and they discuss alternatives. Soha likes one of these, makes the correction on her laptop, and Morgan continues to another word. It's okay. Next, Morgan recasts a collocation error, Soha fixes it, and they move on. Morgan again pauses and Soha points to her screen to explain an idea she is trying to convey; Morgan listens and nods. He spots a place where she has reinforced the idea and commends her for it. Next, a verb tense problem, and he says the tense should be the same as in the preceding sentence. Soha fixes it and decides to scroll to another place to fix a similar mistake. Good catch. Morgan's attention sometimes follows her cursor. Then another recast. Morgan compliments Soha's writing for well-structured paragraphs and having only minor errors. He keeps reading and follows her cursor to another place, reads, pauses, and decides to read aloud a phrase she has written: *previous past.*

Soha looks at the screen, ready to type, but waits. "I'm wondering," he asks, "is there something you were trying to say with *previous past?*" She shakes her head and he explains that it's redundant: "You just need *past.*" She prepares to make a deletion or a note to herself. But he pauses and wonders aloud again about what she might be trying to say; Soha affirms that she means "just *past.*" He says okay and reads on. Then, a change to one part of a sentence requires changes elsewhere. Morgan waits patiently while Soha makes the changes with a bit of Morgan's help. Later, their attention turns to an awkward structure and another tense problem. Then, "*Appreciate the painting with an interest* sounds redundant," the tutor observes. "So maybe just say *appreciate the painting.* Yeah," he says reassuringly as Soha makes the correction. Morgan continues to read aloud: "*His present interest.*" "Does he have only one?" he turns to ask her. Soha hesitates and he asks again, "Does he have just one interest?" but Soha is still confused by the question and asks, "Huh?" For the third attempt, Morgan offers: "*His present interest* makes it sound like he has only <u>one</u> interest, and so I'm wondering . . . (pause)" and finally the writer says, "Oh!" types something, nods, and the session continues on until the appointment time has ended.

From a distance, this session appeared to be engaging for both parties. Gesturing, scrolling, discussing, writing, reading, nodding—it was all there, and the writer seemed satisfied. For his part, Morgan was a very patient tutor who checked for understanding ("Make sense?" "Okay." "Keep going?"). Soha also seemed satisfied afterward when I chatted with her, and she said she planned to continue making edits on her own. In a separate conversation, Morgan said he let Soha's typing and cursor position guide his attention and feedback. He volunteered that he tended to be more directive with graduate writers than with undergraduates, and when I asked about the number and variety of things addressed in the session, he acknowledged there were many. But he said he felt it was more important to concentrate on the paper rather than become sidetracked with word- and sentence-level explanations, which he did not feel terribly confident about providing anyway, as he confided to me afterward.

From one perspective, it is easy to see why the tutor and writer felt this session to be collaborative and productive: Soha controlled the keyboard and pace of the session, and she responded to questions. Morgan asked questions, gave tips, read closely, and gave specific feedback about a variety of items. But upon close observation, this was an editing session without an executive function. There were no goals to define tasks that might result in greater insight and understanding about the student's project or her writing process, and no explicit attention paid to transferring what Soha learned in this session to editing on her own in the future. There was no discussion about how the tutor was spotting errors or what proofreading strategy was being followed. There was no grouping of items and pointing to them as part of a pattern, and no formulating of rules and testing them against Soha's corrections. Missed opportunities abounded, as they always do, but one in particular seemed noteworthy: when Morgan repeated his question about *present interest* even though Soha did not understand it. Perhaps Soha understood the third time or perhaps she pretended to understand so he wouldn't ask her again. Either way, the correction did nothing to help Soha avoid the same problem in the future.

The point here is that, if they are not careful, tutors can use noticing and recasting strategies on a tear, moving so swiftly from one spot to the next that it only *feels* like a lot is being accomplished. In the long run, how much the writer actually retains is anybody's guess. It would be an interesting investigation, in fact, for tutors to study how many recasts writers remember from one time or session to another.

In actual practice, recasts don't always work as planned. The most common breakdown occurs when something like this happens.

> (The student has written, "Last week I write him an e-mail.")
>
> Reading aloud, the tutor pauses and says, "Last week you *wrote* him an e-mail."
>
> The student turns to the tutor and replies, "Yes, because I had to ask him a question."

This is an example of the ways in which modified interactions can sometimes become awkward and even cause minor embarrassment because they catch students off-guard, mistaking a correction for a request for clarification. Directors can help tutors use recasts effectively by teaching them to announce at the beginning of the session that they will use recasts as a tool and inviting writers to decide how tutors will signal that they are about to recast: pausing, saying "hmm," raising a pen, or some other way. As with noticing, framing recasts in this way involves the use of metadiscourse. These discussions are useful because they give writers a greater sense of control in circumstances in which they often feel little control, and they create tools the writer can use and ask for in future tutoring sessions.

Some tutors may be inclined to regard *recast* as another way of saying *rewrite*, but they are not the same thing. A recast presumes an underlying correct form the writer has violated; it also presumes that by producing the correct form, the writer will recall the rule and realize why the correction is needed. A rewrite, on the other hand, involves the tutor's taking control and rewriting something in a way that pleases the tutor. The rewrite may eliminate errors and sound better, but it is not the writer's work and may not be what the writer wants to say or how they want to say it.

There are two gray areas, and they require tutors to recognize differences that aren't always apparent to native speakers. First, when the writer's intended meaning is clear but words and phrases aren't quite "right" sounding, then recasting becomes editing. Tutors must be warned against this misuse of recasting. Sometimes, however, writers benefit from seeing how a more capable peer works with words so they can then try doing it themselves; in this case, recasting a phrase or sentence to achieve a particular goal can be instructive. An example would be times when writers rely on spoken stress to create emphasis instead of placing keywords in emphatic positions that will be recognized in silent reading. In these cases, tutors should explain the goal and give writers a chance to achieve it in their own way. If they can't, recasting may help writers see a way to revise a sentence to improve emphasis, and hopefully such modeling will lead writers to be able to do this revision independently next time or with a bit of help. The warning to tutors here should be that recasting without a goal or a particular form in mind—in other words, recasting for the purpose of making a text sound smoother and more pleasing to the tutor—is generally not advisable.

A second gray area for recasting relates to late-arriving adult learners' difficulties with certain kinds of phrases, like idioms and collocations learned slowly and through experience because they are so numerous they cannot all be taught or memorized. Idioms involve derived sayings like *talking in circles, feeling blue,* and *out of the blue.* Every language has idioms, and learners can often infer their meanings. In fact, difficulty with an idiom can spark an informative discussion about related meanings in both languages. Collocations, on the other hand, are compositional and often domain specific. They are generally better suited for sessions with intermediate and advanced L2 learners. Collocations consist of words that co-occur more often than would be expected by chance. Native speakers of English are usually unaware of how common they are in everyday usage until they make or hear a collocation error. For example: *powerful computer* sounds fine to a native speaker of English, but *strong computer* sounds not quite right. Other examples are *on a budget* (but not *off a budget*) and *crystal clear* (but not *glass clear*). Sometimes second-language learners' collocation "errors" exude pure poetry, like *machine gun wedding* (instead of *shotgun wedding*) and *captured audience* (instead of *captive audience*).

Tutors should be able to recognize certain collocations and be prepared to talk about options, including restating the idea in another way, using the collocation as a native speaker would, or keeping the writer's original formulation. Except for advanced learners and Generation 1.5 students who have had a lot of exposure to colloquial uses of English, collocations are often not available in memory, so it doesn't make sense to coax the writer to recall them. A better idea is to make sure the writing center's resource shelf is stocked with copies of the *Longman Dictionary of Contemporary English* or the *Oxford Collocations Dictionary*, both also available online at http://www.ldoceonline.com/ and http://oxforddictionary.so8848.com/. These resources provide good coverage of collocations, but tutors need to be reminded to use them.

Corrective feedback is an ongoing field of research and provides a path for tutors interested in further study in applied linguistics and composition studies. John Truscott's (1996; Truscott and Hsu 2008) critique of corrective feedback is thought provoking. While Truscott believes errors do not deserve as much attention from teachers as they tend to receive, a more mainstream view (Beason 2001; Bitchener and Ferris 2012; Ferris 2010) is that corrective feedback plays an important role in the overall approach to teaching and learning second-language writing. Dana Ferris's (2002) *Treatment of Error in Second Language Student Writing*, and a more recent volume by John Bitchener and Ferris (2012), provide interesting and accessible overviews of research on corrective feedback in first- and second-language research. However, all research agrees that as writers mature and become more practiced, their errors tend to diminish, and appropriate feedback helps smooth the way.

Corrective feedback responds to specific parts of writers' texts (output) by alerting them to problems and providing comprehensible input that indicates how to repair them. Doing this in a pedagogically sound way begins with knowing what students know and can do on their own, and with knowing that sometimes it is better to introduce new information than to access old. Telling writers what they need to know is a tutor's responsibility. Mehdi Rahimian, a tutor at the University of Manitoba, felt a need to point out the obvious: "When a student does not know the term, sometimes the way we deal with it is to try to induce it, to get it out of their brains. But it doesn't exist in their brains." He became emphatic, saying each word slowly: "It. Is. Not. There. To. Extract. There is nothing to extract!" he said. Then he grew a big smile and added, "When I said this to our tutors, they laughed!" Often the only way to help students understand is to give them the answer, but a tutor's job is to give the answer to the student in a way that stores the information in the brain.

5

PREPARING OURSELVES AND OUR TUTORS

At one time, multilingual writers had a relatively low profile on college campuses in the United States. Now, they are actively recruited by colleges and universities. In some writing centers they comprise more than half the visits; they work as tutors and have become directors. The presence of multilingual writers and tutors has changed the conversation and given all students greater contact with other cultures as these writers have shared their disciplinary, cultural, and personal experiences. As tutors, they offer patience and intelligence to students of all backgrounds. For writing center directors, international students have ushered in a welcome and necessary challenge to English monolingualism. In writing centers around the United States and the world, the challenge is being met most successfully by directors who, through and with their tutors, reach out to writers by taking their needs and aspirations seriously.

Barbara Toth (2012, 7) gives an example of this in something she wrote to her colleagues in the Middle East-North Africa Writing Centers Alliance.

As part of a university founded by King Abdullah of Saudi Arabia and as part of the largest women-only university in the world, the Princess Nora University Writing Studio brings a historic opportunity to build a center created of, by, and for Saudi women that weaves a relationship with other writing centers around the world of, by, and for writing. Western model writing centers do bring certain advantages to sustainability: experienced professional staff, tried and true administrative infrastructure, and best practices based on decades of research and praxis. But the PNU Writing Studio, and those like it, seems poised to contribute something new for writing centers around the world. With less certain advantages may come more definite opportunities to

DOI: 10.7330/9780874219647.c000

capitalize on the necessarily multilingual and multicultural realities of life on the PNU campus.

In this final, brief chapter, I would like to offer remarks and a
few recommendations for the necessarily multilingual and multicultural realities knocking at every writing center's door.

ON PREPARING TUTORS

Educating tutors to work with multilingual writers begins
with writing center directors: Do we ourselves interact with
multilingual students often enough to know their needs and
concerns? Do our tutors have friends who are multilingual
writers? Do we recruit tutors who are multilingual writers or
learning another language? A diverse writing center is, ide-
ally, one whose staff has enough depth and breadth to meet
the needs students present. In the centers I have visited, such
diversity varies. In my own writing center, there is no prevent-
ing the turnover of peer tutors from one semester and year to
the next as they graduate, find better jobs, or move on, so it
is hard to maintain a staff whose members have the range of
backgrounds and talents needed to work with all students who
visit. Nonetheless, it is important to be proactive about diversity and to sustain a vision for what tutors should know and be
able to do.

A recent doctoral dissertation by John Larkin Boyd (2013)
offers such a vision, based on Beaufort's (2007) knowledge
domains of discourse community, subject matter, genre, rhetoric, and writing process. Boyd recommends "that writing centers
might reconceive of their approach to tutor instruction in terms
of expertise by providing three forms of support: a heightened
focus on disciplinary discourse conventions, opportunities for
deliberate practice, and engagement in an evolving process of
mentorship." While he allows that regular staff meetings may be
enough to achieve such a vision with the appropriate instructional approach, he believes a credit-bearing class or internship
is ideal. Moreover, "locating tutor instruction within the academic curriculum . . . establishes the process of tutoring as a

clearly intellectual endeavor, rather than a matter of skills-based or technical training" (Boyd 2013, 172).

Carl Bereiter and Marlene Scardamalia (1993) suggest a way to think about the development of expertise based on what individuals do in the face of constantly changing problems, and they offer two concepts that may be helpful to directors. The first is to reinvest effort, or take whatever lesson is learned in one situation and hold onto it for the future. The other is to seek out problems that don't have ready-made answers. In both cases, the orientation is forward looking and expects encounters with the unknown. Peer-led writing centers are places where this orientation can take root, not because they are filled with tutors who already possess lots of knowledge and skills for tutoring writing—most do not—but because they can attract young talent for whom meeting new problems and feeling at ease with uncertainty come naturally—especially when it comes to learning a new language. So another way to look at tutors' knowledge is to consider their own ambitions for language learning. Tutors who are themselves multilingual or learning another language, or who have significant experience with non-English-speaking cultures, should be among the top candidates for hiring, as the words of one such tutor and writing fellow, Cristine Busser, help to explain:

> I have formally studied French and had a relationship with someone who spoke Spanish with very limited English-speaking skills. My formal training in a Latin-based language helps me to be very in tune to lower-level mistakes made by Spanish-speaking students. Although I could identify these mistakes, as an English speaker, without the experience of studying another language, my studies in French—and the mistakes I make in using French—have prepared me to better explain to students what mistakes they are making, and how not to repeat them. These explanations range from proper sentence structure to appropriate conjugation. My informal training through semiassimilation has helped me especially with explaining spelling mistakes. It is one thing to spell something wrong; it is another to recognize that the student's pronunciation can directly affect how they choose to spell a word. I realize that I am much more aware of an ESL student's struggle to understand the many nuances in the English language.

Except for the United States, schools in most countries—including those with some of the most advanced economies like Austria, Canada, Denmark, Finland, Germany, Luxembourg, the Netherlands, New Zealand, Japan, Korea, and China—have demanding foreign-language education requirements,. In these countries and many other places, English is required in schools at all levels. Other national and regional languages are offered, too. Language instruction in the United States, in contrast, has been in decline, with courses and enrollments down at both the elementary and high-school levels in the last ten years (Jackson and Malone 2009).

As countries around the world continue to advance, so does the power and influence of their people and the languages they speak. In other words, English is expanding—but so are Spanish, Arabic, Chinese, Russian, Hindi, Urdu, Portuguese, Swahili, and other languages. The same is true of the many forms of World Englishes—those varieties of English heard in Nigeria and Kenya, India and Bangladesh, Singapore and Hong Kong. They expand as the world shrinks. At the same time, throughout the United States and the rest of the world, governments and institutions insist, through legislation and tests, on a very thin slice of standardized forms that benefit the privileged few.

The implications of all these changes for writing centers will emerge over time. An important principle to keep in mind is that language belongs to no one but those who use it. The potential for powerful constituencies rests with the students, tutors, and directors who represent them as language users. As Jay Jordan (2012) observes, multilingual users are frequently referred to writing centers, which can function

> to quarantine and/or inoculate students whose language practices diverge from acceptable standards. But despite—or perhaps because of—this position, writing centers can simultaneously be spaces where students' cultural and linguistic differences can be more fully explored than many composition classes allow. For various reasons, it is usually difficult to argue for pedagogical and institutional change from the writing center; however, the

> changing perspectives multilingual users and their language uses
> represent present not just ethical but also pragmatic imperatives
> for change, which may give arguments originating from writing
> center tutors and administrators added weight. (27–28)

One example of pragmatic imperatives for change may be found in online writing centers that help to expand acceptance of world Englishes, according to Sabatino and Rafoth (2012).

In the future, writing centers that thrive will be those whose tutors and directors are flush with multilingual and multicultural knowledge and experience so that when they sit down with speakers and writers from diverse linguistic backgrounds, they can draw upon tools that will help them achieve the goals that bring them to school in the first place. In this construction zone of language, there is hard but satisfying work.

Writing center directors must consider their own knowledge and the curricular resources they can bring to bear on staff education. This responsibility makes deciding what tutors should know a practical matter of figuring out what directors are able to teach them, both on their own and with help from their colleagues. In other words, directors must weigh, and perhaps alter, their own developmental trajectories as well as their tutors'.

Some of the knowledge directors must pay greater attention to in staff education is clear: teaching tutors to make effective use of negotiated interaction as a tool for teaching and learning, raising their awareness of the importance of helping writers learn and use new words, and making them more effective at giving feedback on errors. This book has attempted to increase directors' and tutors' awareness of these topics for staff education and further research. In a recent book chapter, Lauren Fitzgerald (2012), former editor of *The Writing Center Journal*, observes that, despite decades of attention paid to conversation and talk in tutorials, the writing center field has "slim offerings" of research involving discourse analysis (82), with notable exceptions taken up by SLA researchers Williams and Severino (2004) in a special issue of the *Journal of Second Language Writing*, and a more recent investigation by Isabelle Thompson (2009).

As writing center directors pay greater attention to theory and research in the field of second-language acquisition, they will uncover new areas of investigation relevant to their own centers and new learning opportunities for themselves and their tutors.

The knowledge and skills needed to work with multilingual writers may come more naturally to some tutors than others, but all who work in writing centers need more opportunities to get to know the international students on their campuses. Making acquaintances is a first step in the work of preparing to tutor multilingual writers because it affects how tutors and directors do their jobs, and it goes to the heart of one's personal commitment to diversity. Ilona Leki (2009) observed:

> There is also a tendency among humans to see their own social and cultural group as highly nuanced and differentiated but to be less able to fully grasp that all social and cultural groups are equally nuanced and differentiated. . . . But the most effective way for writing center tutors to experience these nuances firsthand is to take advantage of the visits of these multilingual, multicultural individuals to the writing center and show interest in their home language, country, or culture by engaging them in the kind of small talk that usually accompanies tutoring sessions, and so get to know them one by one. (13)

Spoken and written language cohabit in a writing center, equally important but functioning differently. The small talk of ordinary, get-acquainted conversation is key to building a relationship and usually comes easily, while other kinds of talk must be learned and practiced. Metatalk, for example, must be part of the tutor's repertoire, but shifting into it when it is needed does not happen automatically. Tutors tend to rely upon talk that comes naturally or that they have heard from their own teachers, even though a more intentionally instructive approach tailored to the writer's needs would be more helpful. In an essay written more than twenty years ago, Thomas Newkirk (1989) highlighted the importance of the first five minutes in a writing conference and noted that tutors tend to talk too much, filling up the space that writers need to gather their thoughts and express themselves. More recently, Terese Thonus (2002;

2004) and Jo Mackiewicz and Isabelle Thompson (2015) have investigated the discourse of successful tutorials with first- and second-language writers and provided many insights for directors to share with their tutors. Such research helps directors pay attention to when and how talk is used in the beginning, middle, and end of conferences and forms a basis for constructive feedback.

ON NEGOTIATED INTERACTION

The University of Manitoba's Academic Learning Center is located front and center on the main floor in the university's new library. It occupies a space near Starbucks where students gather, laugh, and complain about their courses. "It's a beautiful, cheerful environment," says Kathy Block, the writing services coordinator. I asked Block what issues and concerns she has talked about recently with her tutors, and she said, "We talked about sentence-level help and how much we can give to EAL's," referring to students for whom English is an additional language. She also pointed to restrictions imposed by the university's Policy on Inappropriate Collaboration. "We feel okay to work on the macro or thesis level, but we worry about the sentence level. The policy says you can't give a sentence model, but students need more," she said.

Block is coauthor of *Creating Meaning* (Block et al. 2008), a book to help advanced multilingual students shuttle between reading, critical analysis, vocabulary, and writing. She talked about the ways in which thesis statements, paraphrases, summaries, and other aspects of writing require a juggling of form and meaning. "I'd like consultants to be able to enter into negotiation of meaning by giving options, putting words to a meaning and helping writers get to the language," she said.

As a coordinator, Block meets with new tutors for fourteen hours each fall before they shadow a more experienced tutor and are then tutored themselves. The time devoted to tutor education is jam packed, she says, and it is difficult to find time to work in everything she needs to do. She also observes her tutors frequently and looks at the papers and questions students bring to them. When we spoke, the notions of helping EAL students "put words to meaning" and "get to the language" were ideas she kept coming back to. They resonated with her as she recalled one student, an advanced-level speaker, from China: "She had a good sense of the logical flow of her text and could see connections between ideas. But she struggled on the sentence level," she said.

Block is an English L1 speaker who was born in Canada and studied French in Quebec. For a time she worked at the Center for Indigenous Environmental Resources, helping students from Canada's First Nations population return to their home communities. She directed an intensive-English program at the University of Winnipeg and earned a master's in English as an additional language. "Tutors need basic knowledge of the structure of language," she said. "You have to know what a clause is, to explain what needs to be foregrounded, whether to use *that*—a lot depends on understanding clauses." Continuing on, she seemed to shift topics, but soon I realized we were still talking about form and meaning. "We need to provide input through a rich discussion. Not one that presumes what they mean or want to say, but to help them get there," she stressed. "If you ask students whether they would prefer we tell them what to write or give them options," she said, "they will pick options because they regard the options as bonus information they can use for next time, see?" In other words, Block seemed to say if students' own ideas are the most important thing, as her university's policy on collaboration holds, then tutors must get these ideas to language, and doing that requires rich discussions that move between meaning and form.

As she spoke, another writer came to her mind who had used an online translator. "The meaning was obscure, and we got to talking about how it came about," she said. "Finally, we were able to parse it into three chunks: one, from a textbook; two, a lexical chunk she had learned in a language class at some point—I think it was 'it is noteworthy that'; and three, an online translator." The use of online translators is a reminder that the landscape for teaching and learning literacy has been shifting and will continue to do so. Writing center directors will have to deal with the reality that academic writing in English is, for many students and their teachers here and around the world, not a sacred relic but a tool. "What impressed me," Block said, "was how many strategies the student had used— textbook, language class, and translator. The text was neither fluent nor clear, but she was working really hard and she had drawn on all the resources she had in order to get to language." What writers are likely to learn in and through a writing center will come from the interactions we negotiate with them as they use language to achieve their goals. Negotiating with them about meaning and form is the foundation for helping them use this tool.

Below, we will see how a graduate-student writer majoring in an applied science discipline sat down with a paper she said her professor helped her with, meaning he had mostly written it himself, and which she now wanted to turn into a more fully developed proposal. The student was smart, motivated, and eager to get on with her research project. "What are we going to do?" her tutor wondered after the session, clearly implying the answer was obvious: we are going to take it in stride and help the student get on with her research. The way we tutor is changing, and we are going to adapt. If there is a lesson here for directors, I believe it is to help tutors also learn to use, knowledgeably and intentionally, a greater variety of tools for tutoring—for scaffolding, error feedback, and expanding their own knowledge of language. Using tools depends on having many and discarding them when they don't work. The pages of this book suggest where to look for some of these tools and the reasons they might be effective, but they don't provide a cupboard of strategies to open for tomorrow morning's tutoring session. Instead, the goal of this book, and for staff education generally, has been to broach a pragmatic understanding of areas that deserve greater attention and to encourage directors and tutors to take the necessary steps to help multilingual writers get to language.

ON HANDS BEING ON AND OFF

Writing center directors have traditionally taught tutors to keep their distance and avoid even the appearance of doing students' work for them. Sometimes university policies, as we saw at the University of Manitoba, restrict what tutors can do. Mostly, though, tutors are supposed to use implicit instruction because it is supposed to create authentic, independent learning. Thanks in part to cautions given by Nancy Grimm (1999), Staben and Nordhaus (2009), and others, the writing center community has moved away from the kind of hands-off tutoring that disenfranchises students and withholds insider knowledge, keeping students from nonmainstream cultures on the sidelines and making them guess about what is expected of them. Implicit instruction can frustrate multilingual and minority students because it enacts, as Grimm says, "the belief that what is expected is natural behavior rather than culturally specific performance" (Grimm 1999, 31). Implicit instruction must therefore be handled carefully and with scaffolding so students understand why the effort being demanded of them is worth it.

Lisa Chason has taught in China, Vietnam, and the United States, where she was born. She lived in the Netherlands for twenty years and learned Dutch. She is now working on her doctorate in global education and tutoring in the campus writing center. She is deeply thoughtful about teaching and learning languages. I asked her how learning additional languages and teaching overseas have influenced her tutoring. She paused to think for a moment and then remarked that she had just finished "quite a tutoring session."

> One thing I would say is, sometimes if somebody just tells you what to do, you can make a big shift. In the writing center of course we want to lead the language-learning student to discover the correct form, but sometimes it works to just tell them.
>
> If someone is already high level, like she [her recent tutee] was, then as soon as I said it, she got it. When I was writing Dutch, sometimes it helped *a lot* if someone just showed me. It helped me to see, to fill in spaces between concepts I had learned that I could then reflect on. It was so helpful to just be shown.

The implication for writing center pedagogy is worth considering. In the past, explicit or direct instruction by tutors has tended to spell trouble, but today writing centers are generally more comfortable with a more hands-on approach. The challenge for the future may be to understand why some mentors, teachers, and tutors need to be more directly involved in students' writing than we have realized.

"How directive to be depends on level—level of writing, on how many problems there are in the paper, on how the writer talks about their writing, on so many factors," Chason said. "When she [her client] sat down, she told me, 'My advisor helped me write this abstract.' It was a gorgeous abstract, perfect English. Now, she has to write the full research proposal alone, and we'll see how that goes." Chason observed that the abstract the professor had apparently written functioned like an assignment, a detailed prompt. "The abstract will inform her about what to write, guide her, do all it's supposed to do."

"I mean, what are we gonna do? You know, our students are 'young' when it comes to putting their thoughts into English"— she nods toward the desk where she had just finished the session—"but they're mature when it comes to migratory birds in interstitial environments in large cities—the topic my earlier Korean student brought in."

To say we help writers learn to write in English seems straightforward enough until we encounter teachers and mentors who deliver on that promise in ways strikingly different from our own. Chason is an expert in language education, and the force of her question *what are we gonna do?* poses a clear challenge to received wisdom and a call to adapt to the ways people use writing around the world. But adapt to what, exactly, and how?

Helping writers learn to write in English also means helping them learn something useful and appropriate to their needs and aspirations. To do this, tutors must possess a base of knowledge that helps them recognize what the learner already knows. This step and the next one are often the most difficult. Chason believes, from her own experience as a learner and a teacher, that there are times when the thing learners need most is someone to *show* them, tell them directly what they are missing. When this idea is elevated to a meeting between a student and her graduate advisor, the result is sometimes a gorgeous abstract, which itself is a mere peephole into the entire work. Does it matter so terribly much who claims authorship of it?

Disciplines and occupations have their own ideas about writing because writing is not owned by English or any one discipline. Nor is it owned by institutional policies or copyright legislation. Like language itself, it is "owned" by those who use it, and most who use it see it see writing as a tool: writing is facts, contracts, proposals—and almost anything you want it to be. So long as writing gets to the result, whatever it is, it's good enough because the more important work and underlying values lie elsewhere.

Stephen North (1984) fretted that utilitarian views of writing cause writing centers to be treated as "the grammar and drill center, the fix-it shop, the first aid station" (37). For a time, it seemed the field ran so far away from such characterizations that it forgot who writing centers served and why those writers came there. For example, multilingual writers visited writing centers well before they appeared in the literature of the field. Directors have since moved to correct the imbalance by helping tutors become more involved pedagogically with writers and writing, even as ideas about texts and authorship evolve: a professor writes a student's abstract and she comes to the writing center to work on the full proposal. A multilingual writing center ought to be able to handle that.

ON REACHING OUT TO FACULTY

At the faculty workshop for working with ESL students at the University of Illinois Urbana-Champaign, a group of instructors, teaching associates, and program coordinators from across campus are gathered in a classroom in Lincoln Hall, located on the main quad. Since its dedication in 1913, Lincoln Hall has undergone three renovations, the latest completed in 2013. A bronze bust of President Abraham Lincoln and a tablet of the

Gettysburg Address still overlook the main foyer, but the building now has new lighting, wifi, and multimedia classrooms. The renovation used sustainable design and green construction materials—rooftop plantings, recycled tiles, and environmentally safe paints, adhesives, fibers, and refrigerants. The workshop leaders, Yu-Kyung Kang, Andrea Olinger, and Paul Prior open with a reflective writing and discussion activity, and as the workshop unfolds, the leaders address a few related topics and issues, including the various labels used to refer to second-language writers and what they signify. They refer to Dana Ferris's (2009) *Teaching College Writing to Diverse Student Populations* and draw upon this and other scholarship in the field of second-language writing.

At one point in the discussion, the leaders jump to a slide containing this quotation: "Sophisticated language development ultimately requires long-term communicative engagement in the relevant communities of the target language users. Thus practices that increase engagement and use of language are the best ways to promote language development." The words seem apt for a group of instructors whose conceptual vocabulary for working with and talking about second-language writers and writing is developing, too. Like the multilingual students they teach, when it comes to learning something new, there is a limit to what they can discern through common sense, intuition, and reflections on practice. Once they have tapped these resources, they stand to benefit from learning new information, engaging new concepts, and enacting new skills in response to expert feedback.

Yu-Kyung Kang draws from her experience as a PhD candidate, the advisor for the Korean Student Association, and the assistant director of the UIUC Writers' Workshop. Andrea Olinger is assistant director of the Center for Writing Studies and a PhD candidate in writing studies. They work as a team, introducing ideas and fielding questions: How much accented writing should I accept? Are you saying that marking up all the errors in a paper . . . well, does that do *any* good? How do I know which errors are "untreatable"?

These are but some of the questions instructors have when they begin to think through what it means to read and respond to their students' writing. Libbie Morley directs the UIUC Writers Workshop and creates opportunities to meet and talk about multilingual writers—with librarians, teaching assistants, writing-across-the-curriculum faculty, MBA tutors, and others. It helps that the Writers Workshop is part of the Center for Writing Studies, whose graduate students work and conduct research in the workshop, but Morley also extends her reach across the campus, wherever multilingual writers and their instructors could benefit from assistance through the Writers Workshop.

One of Morley's consultants, John O'Connor, described a frustrating semester for consultants when multilingual students who were enrolled in certain courses taught by teaching associates in one college descended on the workshop. It appeared their instructors had decided to take a get-tough approach with the students' writing, and for them this meant grades heavily weighted against surface errors. "Students were in various levels of distress," he recalled, "though the content of their work was strong." He noted that Morley met with the instructors in that college and then with the center's tutors to coordinate efforts and address the problem. "We addressed the errors with students and helped them track their progress. Discussions of rules of grammar were very helpful, even empowering, for them—especially when the consultants ceded expertise to the students. Maintaining the interactive nature of sessions was really important." O'Connor explained how he drew upon his experience as a second-language conversation tutor overseas while he was working on his master's degree in ESL.

A large research university like UIUC is fortunate to have experts to respond to issues like this. Not all colleges and universities have second-language writing specialists and experienced ESL tutors on hand to step in, or to provide consultations. But small schools need not feel isolated. Writing center directors in all schools can team up with faculty in other departments, community literacy workers, and outside experts. They can form reading groups and reflect on their own practices. They can attend conferences and conduct action research with their tutors. A former editor of the *Writing Center Journal,* Lauren Fitzgerald advises, "To find your own direction, look for the current assumptions and controversies in your center, among your colleagues, and in professional conversations, and also look for the gaps in the knowledge circulating in these contexts. Once you have found your exigence, read widely in the scholarship about your topic with an aim of entering the conversation and moving this conversation forward" (Fitzgerald 2012, 87). By looking outside the center at scholarship and research, as well as looking inside their own writing centers with a critical eye, directors and tutors can outline the issues facing their writing centers and find ways to deal with them.

CONCLUSION

Writing centers have a long history, but present-day writing centers are by and large the product of a period of change in higher education in the 1970s and 1980s that saw growing student populations, an influx of nontraditional learners, and the perception that higher education had become irrelevant to a rapidly changing world. The writing centers of this decade have seen changes that could be described in this way too, but the similarities are superficial. Thirty and forty years ago, the population of higher education was changing, but unlike today, this change was driven by the postwar baby boom that came of age in the 1970s and '80s. Like today, there was an influx of nontraditional learners, but unlike today they were mostly adults returning to school and first-generation college students. And the perception of irrelevance had much to do with social unrest related to the American civil rights movement of the 1960s, protests against the war in Vietnam, and social and political campaigns against crime, poverty, and inequality. Harvey S. Wiener (1986) observed that in the 1970s and '80s, these changes, along with a perceived decline in reading and writing skills, undermined confidence in traditional ways of teaching. Education leaders responded by promoting alternative approaches, and writing centers were one of the alternatives. They found space to occupy and developed a student-centered ethos that was peer led, welcoming, and decidedly unclassroomlike. They also conformed to institutional and societal expectations, which included a stable and static English monolingualism tied to Standard American Edited English, and to then-prevailing ideas about authorship, texts, media, and technology.

Today's notions of authorship, texts, media, and technology bear little resemblance to those that seemed so secure only a few decades ago, but schools and writing centers are coming around. For example, the ease with which information is found, shared, and repurposed is forcing directors and tutors to reexamine the rights of student authors versus corporations that profit from freshman essays (Brown et al. 2007). Moreover, the presence of so many nonnative speakers of English on campus has pushed linguistic diversity to center stage in staff meetings and professional publications. Their presence has, among other things, required directors and tutors to rethink what they know about their own language, learning languages, and academic discourse generally. This book has tried to show how and why such rethinking is good for those who work in writing centers and the reasons it needs to accelerate.

But while looking at several decades of history helps to explain how today's writing centers came to be and how they must change, it would be a mistake to conclude that writing centers simply need to refine their practices to keep up with the times. This book has also tried to show that a more fundamental orientation to the role of tutoring is necessary. Instead of tutors automatically easing into the comfort zone of nondirectiveness, collaboration, and confidence boosting, which comes readily enough to native speakers of English in a monolingual environment, directors and tutors must anticipate what knowledge, information, and skills are needed in order to function in a multilingual context. This means tutors must be prepared well beyond what comes naturally to an earnest, well-read, and verbal native speaker. It means they must be familiar with structural perspectives of language and discourse, the syntax of clauses, and the modifications to normal conversational interaction that create opportunities for teaching and learning. It also means they must become comfortable and familiar with the new faces of the students themselves. In addition to seeing the work of writing centers as taking place at a desk or table, tutors must get to know their classmates who are different from them and explore their new languages and customs with them.

Looking back, we may find that Kenneth Bruffee, despite his important contributions to the creation and progress of writing centers, overlooked a critical component—the knowledge of individual tutors. When Bruffee sized up the problem with American higher education, he concluded that students needed "not an extension of but an alternative to traditional classroom teaching" (Bruffee 1984b, 86). In other words, Bruffee believed that by modeling instruction on a good conversation between peers rather than a stale lecture from an authority figure, learners would be inspired enough to keep advancing, by themselves and with one another. Exactly how new information was to be obtained, or where and how individual learners were supposed to encounter it, did not occupy much of Bruffee's attention. His embrace of one set of research findings is telling in this regard.

In his classic article published in *College English* in 1984 and again in his book in 1999, Bruffee seized on data obtained by M. L. K. Abercrombie (1960), who investigated medical students doing hospital rounds with their teaching physician. Abercrombie found that when medical students worked as a group instead of working alone, they made better patient diagnoses because they acquired medical judgment faster. Bruffee concluded that collaborative learning "harnessed the powerful educative force of peer influence that has been—and largely still is—ignored and hence wasted by traditional forms of education" (Bruffee 1984a, 638). He abhorred the dullness and exclusion of rote methods and focused on learners' harnessing positive social influences "by challenging each other's biases and presuppositions; by negotiating collectively toward new paradigms of perceptions, thoughts, feelings, and expressions; and by joining larger, more experienced communities of knowledgeable peers through assenting to those communities' interests, values, languages, and paradigms of perceptions and thoughts" (Bruffee 1999, 646). Bruffee had little to say about the source of individual learning among the medical students Abercrombie studied. In other words, before these medical students could prove the undisputed value of working together, they must have had to do what is required of all medical students—learn and commit to memory facts, theories, case studies, ideas, and other information.

Absent from Bruffee's discussion, and from many of the ensuing discussions, is where tutors are supposed to get the new knowledge they are expected to have at their disposal when they assist students and collaborate with other tutors in the writing center. In writing centers in the past, monolingual assumptions about English meant that monolingual tutors did not have to stretch as far as they do today. The gap between what tutors already knew and what they needed to learn, once they began attending staff meetings and gaining experience, was more easily surmounted. But now in the United States, with growing numbers of minority and multilingual college students, tutors encounter writers who speak a wider variety of languages, including varieties of English, than writing center tutors were accustomed to seeing in years past. Today's students require tutors who are prepared for such diversity and who have the knowledge and skills to help multicultural and multilingual writers meet their goals of improving their written English.

While this book argues for changes in the ways we prepare tutors to assist multilingual writers, it is just as important to remember that multilingual writers will drive many of these changes themselves. They will continue to ask tutors hard questions about linguistic rules and discourse patterns, and about why something is or is not correct. This is as it should be, and directors and tutors will need to respond by learning to provide complete and sensible if somewhat imperfect answers. Fortunately, one question directors and tutors will never be able to answer, especially once they get to know their multilingual writers, is who benefits more—tutors, or the writers they assist?

GLOSSARY

automaticity. The ability to speak or write in a second language without worrying about low-level details such as correct pronunciation or thinking of the right words. Automatic speech flows smoothly and seemingly without a lot of effort.

code gloss. A gloss or brief definition of a key term to aid in comprehension.

comprehensible input. Language a learner can understand.

comprehensible output hypothesis. The idea that second-language learning requires learners to speak and write comprehensibly so that they gain practice and feedback.

depersonalization. A style of discourse that avoids using personal pronouns or naming human actors: "Acceptance of responsibility is a must" is a depersonalized rendering of "someone must accept responsibility."

ELL. English-language learner.

error. An incorrect use of language resulting from the speaker's insufficient knowledge of the correct form (compare *mistake*).

exemplification. An example given to help illustrate something (compare *reformulation*).

fossilization. A persistent state of language acquisition in which little change occurs despite instruction, feedback, and practice.

input. Whatever a language learner hears or sees that is spoken or written in the immediate environment.

interlanguage. A learner's second language while it is still being learned.

L2. An abbreviation for any language learned after the first language (L1).

lexical density. The relative frequency of difficult or unfamiliar words in a text.

metatext. Writing that focuses on the text itself, such as an overview provided for the reader.

mistake. An incorrect use of language that occurs when the speaker knows the correct form but doesn't use it, usually because of inattention (compare *error*).

modified interaction. An intentional change in a conversation's normal pattern in order to teach or point something out, such as slowing or pausing in order to call attention to something.

negative transfer. An error made in one's second language because of the influence of one's first language, such as omitting an article because it would not be used in the speaker's L1 (compare *positive transfer*).

nominalization. A word derived from a verb, adjective, or adverb and used as a noun, such as extract → extraction.

noticing. A second-language teaching strategy aimed at getting learners to focus their attention or notice something specific about using language (compare *modified interaction*).

output. Whatever a language learner writes or says (compare *comprehensible output hypothesis*).

positive transfer. Use of a correct form in the learner's second language resulting from the influence of their first language, such as using an article because it would also be used in the speaker's L1 (compare *negative transfer*).

pushed output. A second-language teaching strategy aimed at getting the learner to speak or write as a way to promote practice and feedback.

recast. A second-language teaching strategy that involves correcting an error by repeating it in its correct form.

reformulation. An explanatory or clarifying phrase, usually signaled by "in other words" or "that is."

REFERENCES

Abercrombie, M. L. J. 1960. *The Anatomy of Judgment*. London: Hutchinson.

Babcock, Rebecca Day, and Terese Thonus. 2012. *Researching the Writing Center: Towards an Evidence-Based Practice*. New York: Peter Lang.

Bawarshi, Anis, and Stephanie Pelkowski. 1999. "Postcolonialism and the Idea of a Writing Center." *Writing Center Journal* 19 (2): 41–58.

Bean, Janet, Maryann Cucchiara, Robert Eddy, Peter Elbow, Rhonda Grego, Rich Haswell, Patricia Irvine, Eileen Kennedy, Ellie Kutz, Al Lehner, and Paul Kei Matsuda. 2011. "Shall We Invite Students to Write in Home Languages? Complicating the Yes/No Debate." In *Second-Language Writing in the Composition Classroom: A Critical Sourcebook*, edited by Paul Kei Matsuda, Michelle Cox, Jay Jordan, and Christina Ortmeier-Hooper, 225–239. Urbana, IL: NCTE/Bedford St. Martin's.

Beason, Larry. 2001. "Ethos and Error: How Business People React to Errors." *College Composition and Communication* 53 (1): 33–64. http://dx.doi.org/10.2307/359061.

Beaufort, Anne. 2007. *College Writing and Beyond*. Logan: Utah State University Press.

Bereiter, Carl, and Marlene Scardamalia. 1993. *Surpassing Ourselves: An Inquiry into the Nature and Implications of Expertise*. Chicago: Open Court.

Berko Gleason, J. 2005. *The Development of Language*. 6th ed. London: Allyn & Bacon.

Bitchener, John, and Dana R. Ferris. 2012. *Written Corrective Feedback in Second Language Acquisition and Writing*. New York: Routledge.

Blau, Susan, John Hall, and Sarah Sparks. 2002. "Guilt-Free Tutoring: Rethinking How We Tutor Non-Native-English-Speaking Students." *Writing Center Journal* 23 (1): 23–44.

Block, Kathy, Laurie Blass, and Hannah Friessen. 2008. *Creating Meaning: Advanced Reading and Writing*. New York: Oxford.

Bongaerts, Theo 1999. "Ultimate Attainment in L2 Pronunciation: The Case of Very Advanced Late L2 Learners." In *Second Language Acquisition and the Critical Period Hypothesis*, edited by David Birdsong, 133–160. Mawah, NJ: Erlbaum.

Boyd, John L. 2013. "Writing Centers and the Problem of Expertise: Knowing and Doing in Peer Tutoring." PhD Diss., Indiana University of Pennsylvania. ProQuest (AAT 3604277).

Bradsher, Keith. 2013. "In China, Betting It All on a Child in College." *New York Times*, February 17, sec. A.

Brereton, John C. 1995. *The Origins of Composition Studies in the American College, 1875–1925*. Pittsburgh, PA: University of Pittsburgh Press.

Brown, Renee, Brian Fallon, Elizabeth Matthews, and Elizabeth Mintie. 2007. "Taking on Turnitin: Tutors Advocating Change." *Writing Center Journal* 27 (1): 7–28.

DOI: 10.7330/9780874219647.c006

Bruffee, Kenneth A. 1984a. "Collaborative Learning and the 'Conversation of Mankind.'" *College English* 46 (7): 635–52. http://dx.doi.org/10.2307/376924.

Bruffee, Kenneth A. 1984b. "Peer Tutoring and the 'Conversation of Mankind.'" In *Writing Centers: Theory and Administration*, edited by Gary A. Olson, 3–15. Urbana, IL: NCTE.

Bruffee, Kenneth. 1999. *Collaborative Learning: Higher Education, Interdependence, and the Authority of Knowledge.* 2nd ed. Baltimore: Johns Hopkins University Press.

Byrd, Patricia. 2005. "Instructed Grammar." In *Handbook of Research in Second Language Teaching and Learning*, edited by Eli Hinkel, 545–61. Mahwah, NJ: Erlbaum.

Canagarajah, A. Suresh. 1993. "Critical Ethnography of a Sri Lankan Classroom: Ambiguities in Student Opposition to Reproduction through ESOL." *TESOL Quarterly* 27 (4): 601–26. http://dx.doi.org/10.2307/3587398.

Canagarajah, A. Suresh. 2002. *The Geopolitics of Academic Writing.* Pittsburgh, PA: University of Pittsburgh Press.

Canagarajah, A. Suresh. 2005. "Critical Pedagogy in L2 Learning and Teaching." In *Handbook of Research in Second Language Teaching and Learning*, edited by Eli Hinkel. Mahwah, NJ: Erlbaum.

Canagarajah, A. Suresh. 2006a. "Toward a Writing Pedagogy of Shuttling between Languages: Learning from Multilingual Writers." *College English* 68 (6): 589–604. http://dx.doi.org/10.2307/25472177.

Canagarajah, A. Suresh. 2006b. "The Place of World Englishes in Composition: Pluralization Continued." *College Composition and Communication* 57 (4): 586–619.

Canagarajah, A. Suresh. 2009. "The Plurilingual Tradition and the English Language in South Asia." *AILA Review* 22:5–22. http://dx.doi.org/10.1075/aila.22.02can.

Carver, Ronald P. 1994. "Percentage of Unknown Vocabulary Words in Text as a Function of the Relative Difficulty of the Text: Implications for Instruction." *Journal of Reading Behavior* 26 (4): 413–37.

Center for Academic Writing. 2004. www.coventry.ac.uk/study-at-coventry/student-support/academic-support/centre-for-academic-writing/. Coventry, UK: Coventry University.

Chauhan, Chetan. 2012. "200 Universities across India in Next 5 Years: Sibal." *Hindustan Times*, April 25. http://www.hindustantimes.com/HTNext/Education/200-universities-across-India-in-next–5-yrs-Sibal/Article1-846073.aspx.

Cogie, Jane. 2006. "ESL Student Participation in Writing Center Sessions." *Writing Center Journal* 26 (2): 48–66.

Condon, Frankie. 2012. *I Hope I Join the Band: Narrative, Affiliation, and Antiracist Rhetoric.* Logan: Utah State University Press.

Conference on College Composition and Communication. 2009 (CCCC). "CCCC Statement on Second Language Writing and Writers." http://www.ncte.org/cccc/resources/positions/secondlangwriting.

Cook, Vivian. 1999. "Going Beyond the Native Speaker in Language Teaching." *TESOL Quarterly* 33 (2): 185–209. http://dx.doi.org/10.2307/3587717.

Cox, Michelle, Jay Jordan, Christina Ortmeier-Hooper, and Gwen Gray Schwartz, eds. 2011. *Reinventing Identities in Second Language Writing.* Urbana, IL: National Council of Teachers of English.

Coxhead, Averil. 2006. *Essentials of Teaching Academic Vocabulary.* Stamford, CT: Cenage.

Cumming, Alister, and Sufumi So. 1996. "Tutoring Second Language Text Revision: Does the Approach to Instruction or the Language of Communication Make a Difference?" *Journal of Second Language Writing* 5 (3): 197–226. http://dx.doi.org/10.1016/S1060-3743(96)90002-8.

Daiute, Colette, and Bridget Dalton. 1985. "'Let's Brighten It Up a Bit': Collaboration and Cognition in Writing." In *The Social Construction of Written Communication,* edited by Bennett A. Rafoth and Donald L. Rubin, 249–269. Norwood, NJ: Ablex.

Denny, Harry. 2010. *Facing the Center: Toward an Identity Politics of One-to-One Mentoring.* Logan: Utah State University Press.

Dudley-Evans, Tony, and Maggie Jo St. John. 1998. *Developments in English for Specific Purposes.* New York: Cambridge.

Emerson, Lisa. 2012. "Developing a 'Kiwi' Writing Centre at Massey University, New Zealand." In *Writing Programs Worldwide: Profiles of Academic Writing in Many Places,* edited by Chris Thaiss, Gerd Bräuer, Paula Carlino, Lisa Ganobcsik-Williams, and Aparna Sinha, 313–323. Fort Collins, CO: WAC Clearinghouse.

Fallon, Brian. 2010. "The Perceived, Conceived, and Lived Experiences of 21st Century Peer Writing Tutors." PhD diss., Indiana University of Pennsylvania. ProQuest (AAT 3433440).

Ferris, Dana R. 2002. *Treatment of Error in Second Language Student Writing.* Ann Arbor, MI: University of Michigan Press.

Ferris, Dana R. 2009. *Teaching College Writing to Diverse Student Populations.* Ann Arbor, MI: University of Michigan Press.

Ferris, Dana R. 2010. "Second Language Writing Research and Written Corrective Feedback in SLA: Intersections and Practical Applications." *Studies in Second Language Acquisition* 32 (02): 181–201. http://dx.doi.org/10.1017/S0272263109990490.

Fitzgerald, Lauren. 2012. "Writing Center Scholarship: A 'Big Cross-Disciplinary Tent.'" In *Exploring Composition Studies: Sites, Issues and Perspectives,* edited by Kelly Ritter and Paul Kei Matsuda. Logan: Utah State University Press.

Fiumara, Gemma Corradi. 1990. *The Other Side of Language: A Philosophy of Listening.* London: Routledge.

García, Ofelia. 2010. "Latino Language Practices and Literacy Education in the US" In *Ethnolinguistic Diversity and Education,* edited by Marcia Farr, Lisya Seloni, and Juyoung Song. New York: Routledge.

García, Ofelia, Jo Anne Kleifgen, and Lorraine Falchi. 2008. "From English Language Learners to Emergent Bilinguals." In *Equity Matters: Research Review No. 1,* 7–59. New York: Teachers College, Columbia University.

Gass, Susan. 1997. *Input, Interaction, and the Second Language Learner.* Mahwah, NJ: Erlbaum.

Gass, Susan, and Evangeline Varonis. 1985. "Variation in Native Speaker Speech Modification to Non-Native Speakers." *Studies in Second Language Acquisition* 7 (1): 37–57. http://dx.doi.org/10.1017/S0272263100005143.

Gass, Susan, and Evangeline Varonis. 1991. "Miscommunication in Nonnative Speaker Discourse." In *"Miscommunication" and Problematic Talk,* edited by

Nikolas Coupland, Howard Giles, and John M. Wiemann. Newbury Park, CA: Sage.

Geller, Anne E., Michele Eodice, Frankie Condon, Meg Carroll, and Elizabeth H. Boquet, eds. 2007. *The Everyday Writing Center.* Logan: Utah State University Press.

Greenfield, Laura, and Karen Rowan, eds. 2011. *Writing Centers and the New Racism: A Call for Sustainable Dialogue and Change.* Logan: Utah State University Press.

Grimm, Nancy. 1999. *Good Intentions: Writing Center Work for Postmodern Times.* Portsmouth, NH: Boynton/Cook.

Halliday, M. A. K., and Ruqayia Hasan. 1976. *Cohesion in English.* London: Longman.

Halliday, M. A. K., and Ruqaiya Hasan. 1989. *Language, Context and Text: Aspects of Language in a Social Semiotic Perspective.* Oxford, UK: Oxford University Press.

Halstead, Isabella. 1975. "Putting Error in Its Place." *Journal of Basic Writing* 1 (1): 72–86.

Harris, Muriel, and Tony Silva. 1993. "Tutoring ESL Students: Issues and Options." *College Composition and Communication* 44 (4): 525–37. http://dx.doi.org/10.2307/358388.

Holliday, Adrian R. 1999. "Small Cultures." *Applied Linguistics* 20 (2): 237–64. http://dx.doi.org/10.1093/applin/20.2.237.

Holliday, Adrian R. 2005. *The Struggle to Teach English as an International Language.* Oxford, UK: Oxford University Press.

Holliday, Adrian R. 2006. "Native-Speakerism." *ELT Journal* 60 (4): 385–87. http://dx.doi.org/10.1093/elt/ccl030.

Horner, Bruce, Min-Zhan Lu, and Paul Kei Matsuda, eds. 2010. *Cross-Language Relations in Composition.* Carbondale: Southern Illinois University Press.

Hsueh-chao, Marcella, and Paul Nation. 2000. "Unknown Vocabulary Density and Reading Comprehension." *Reading in a Foreign Language* 13 (1): 403–30.

Huang, Tung-chiou. 2010. "The Application of Translingualism to Language Revitalization in Taiwan." *Asian Social Science* 6 (2): 44–59. http://www.ccse net.org/journal/index.php/ass.

Hudson, R. A. 1996. *Sociolinguistics.* New York: Cambridge. http://dx.doi.org /10.1017/CBO9781139166843.

Hutchison, Tom, and Alan Waters. 1987. *English for Specific Purposes.* New York: Cambridge. http://dx.doi.org/10.1017/CBO9780511733031.

Hyland, Kenneth. 2004. *Disciplinary Discourses: Social Interactions in Academic Writing.* New York: Longman.

Hyland, Kenneth. 2005. *Metadiscourse.* London: Continuum International.

Hyland, Kenneth. 2007. "Applying a Gloss: Exemplifying and Reformulating in Academic Discourse." *Applied Linguistics* 28 (2): 266–85. http://dx.doi.org /10.1093/applin/amm011.

Hyland, Kenneth. 2009. *Academic Discourse.* London: Continuum International.

Ioup, Georgette, Elizabeth Boustagui, Manal El Tigi, and Martha Mosell. 1994. "Reexamining the Critical Period Hypothesis." *Studies in Second Language Acquisition* 16 (1): 73–98. http://dx.doi.org/10.1017/S0272263100012596.

Irvine, Patricia, and Nan Elsasser. 1988. "The Ecology of Literacy: Negotiating Writing Standards in a Caribbean Setting." In *The Social Construction of*

Written Communication, edited by Ben Rafoth and Donald L. Rubin, 304–320. Norwood, NJ: Ablex.

Jackson, Frederic H., and Margaret E. Malone. 2009. *Building the Foreign Language Capacity We Need: Toward a Comprehensive Strategy for a National Language Framework.* Washington, DC: Center for Applied Linguistics.

Jordan, Jay. 2012. *Redesigning Composition for Multilingual Realities.* Urbana, IL: NCTE.

Kail, Harvey. 1983. "Collaborative Learning in Context: The Problem with Peer Tutoring." *College English* 45 (6): 594–9. http://dx.doi.org/10.2307/377146.

Kail, Harvey, and John Trimbur. 1987. "The Politics of Peer Tutoring." *Writing Center Journal* 11 (1–2): 5–12.

Krashen, Stephen. 1982. *Principles and Practice in Second Language Acquisition.* Oxford, UK: Pergamon.

Krashen, Stephen. 1985. *The Input Hypothesis: Issues and Implications.* London: Longman.

Leki, Iona. 2007. *Undergraduates in a Second Language.* New York: Taylor & Francis.

Leki, Ilona. 2009. "Before the Conversation: A Sketch of Some Possible Backgrounds, Experiences, and Attitudes among ESL Students Visiting a Writing Center." In *ESL Writers: A Guide for Writing Center Tutors*, edited by Shanti Bruce and Ben Rafoth. Portsmouth, NH: Boynton/Cook.

Leung, Constant, Roxy Harris, and Ben Rampton. 1997. "The Idealised Native Speaker, Reified Ethnicities, and Classroom Realities." *TESOL Quarterly* 31 (3): 543–60. http://dx.doi.org/10.2307/3587837.

Lightbown, Patsy M., and Nina Spada. 2006. *How Languages Are Learned.* 3rd ed. Oxford, UK: Oxford University Press.

Linville, Cynthia. 2009. "Editing Line by Line." In *ESL Writers: A Guide for Writing Center Tutors.* 2nd ed. Edited by Shanti Bruce and Ben Rafoth, 116–31. Portsmouth, NH: Heinemann.

Liu, Pei-hsun Emma. 2010. "White Prestige Ideology, Identity and Investment: ESL Composition Class as a Site of Resistance and Accommodation for Taiwanese Students." PhD diss., Indiana University of Pennsylvania. ProQuest (AAT 3403196).

Lloyd, Marion. 2010. "Mexico's Universities Struggle to Respond to Demand for Degrees." *Chronical of Higher Education*, July 5. http://chronicle.com/article/Mexicos-Universities-Struggle/66143/.

Long, Michael. 1981. "Input, Interaction, and Second Language Acquisition." *Annals of the New York Academy of Sciences* 379: 259–78. http://dx.doi.org/10.1111/j.1749-6632.1981.tb42014.x.

Long, Michael. 1983. "Native Speaker / Non-Native Speaker Conversation and the Negotiation of Comprehensible Input." *Applied Linguistics* 4 (2): 126–41. http://dx.doi.org/10.1093/applin/4.2.126.

Lotbinière, Max de. 2011. "South Korean Parents Told: Pre-School English 'Harmful.'" *The Guardian Weekly*, November 8. http://www.theguardian.com/education/2011/nov/08/south-korea-english-teaching-fears.

Lu, Min-Zhan, and Bruce Horner. 2013. "Translingual Literacy, Language Difference, and Matters of Agency." *College English* 75 (6): 582–607.

Mackiewicz, Jo. 2015. *Talking About Writing*. New York: Routledge.

Master, Peter. 2005. "Research in English for Specific Purposes." In *Handbook of Research in Second Language Teaching and Learning*, edited by Eli Hinkel, 99–115. Mahwah, NJ: Erlbaum.

Matsuda, Aya, and Paul Kei Matsuda. 2010. "World Englishes and the Teaching of Writing." *TESOL Quarterly* 44 (2): 369–74. http://dx.doi.org/10.5054/tq.2010.222222.

Matsuda, Paul Kei. 2006. "The Myth of Linguistic Homogeneity in U.S. College Composition." *College English* 68 (6): 637–51. http://dx.doi.org/10.2307/25472180.

Matsuda, Paul Kei. 2012. "Teaching Composition in the Multilingual World." In *Exploring Composition Studies: Sites, Issues and Perspectives*, edited by Kelly Ritter and Paul Kei Matsuda. Logan: Utah State University Press.

Matsuda, Paul Kei, and Michelle Cox. 2009. "Reading an ESL Writer's Text." In *ESL Writers: A Guide for Writing Center Tutors*. 2nd ed, edited by Shanti Bruce and Ben Rafoth. Portsmouth: Boynton/Cook.

McMurtrie, Beth. 2012. "China Continues to Drive Foreign-Student Growth in the United States." *Chronicle of Higher Education*, November 12. http://chronicle.com/article/China-Continues-to-Drive/135700/.

Metcalf, Alan A. 1979. *Chicano English*. Arlington, VA: Center for Applied Linguistics.

Mignolo, Walter D. 1996. "Linguistic Maps, Literary Geographies, and Cultural Landscapes: Languages, Languaging, and (Trans)nationalism." *Modern Language Quarterly* 57 (2): 181–96. http://dx.doi.org/10.1215/00267929-57-2-181.

Nakamaru, Sarah. 2010. "Lexical Issues in Writing Center Tutorials with International and US-Educated Multilingual Writers." *Journal of Second Language Writing* 19 (2): 95–113. http://dx.doi.org/10.1016/j.jslw.2010.01.001.

Nation, I. S. P. 2001. *Learning Vocabulary in Another Language*. Cambridge, UK: Cambridge University Press. http://dx.doi.org/10.1017/CBO9781139524759.

Nation, I. S. P. 2006. "How Large a Vocabulary Is Needed for Reading and Listening?" *Canadian Modern Language Review* 63 (1): 59–82. http://dx.doi.org/10.3138/cmlr.63.1.59.

Nation, Paul, and Jonathan Newton. 1997. *Second Language Vocabulary Acquisition*, edited by James Coady and Thomas Huckin, 238–54. New York: Cambridge.

Newkirk, Thomas. 1989. "The First Five Minutes: Setting the Agenda in a Writing Conference." In *Writing and Response: Theory, Practice, Research*, edited by Chris Anson, 317–331. Urbana, IL: NCTE.

North, Stephen M. 1984. "The Idea of a Writing Center." *College English* 46 (5): 433–46. http://dx.doi.org/10.2307/377047.

Peirce, Bronwyn Norton. 1989. "Toward a Pedagogy of Possibility in the Teaching of English Internationally: People's English is South Africa." *TESOL Quarterly* 23 (3): 401–20. http://dx.doi.org/10.2307/3586918.

Pennycook, Alastair. 2001. *Critical Applied Linguistics: An Introduction*. Mahwah, NJ: Erlbaum.

Phillipson, Robert 1992. *Linguistic Imperialism*. Oxford, UK: Oxford University Press.

Polio, Charlene. 2012. "The Relevance of Second Language Acquisition Theory to the Written Error Correction Debate." *Journal of Second Language Writing* 21: 375–89. http://dx.doi.org/10.1016/j.jslw.2012.09.004.

Rafoth, Ben. 2009. "English for Those Who (Think They) Already Know It." In *ESL Writers: A Guide for Writing Center Tutors.* 2nd ed. Edited by Shanti Bruce and Ben Rafoth. Portsmouth, NH: Boynton/Cook.

Reid, Joy. 2011. "'Eye' Learners and 'Ear' Learners: Identifying the Needs of International Students and U.S. Resident Writers." In *Second-Language Writing in the Composition Classroom: A Critical Sourcebook,* edited by Paul Kei Matsuda, Michelle Cox, Jay Jordan, and Christina Ortmeier-Hooper, 76–88. Urbana, IL: NCTE/Bedford St. Martin's.

Reigstad, Thomas J., and Donald A. McAndrew. 1984. *Training Tutors for Writing Conferences.* Urbana, IL: NCTE.

Ritter, Jennifer. 2002. "Negotiating the Center: An Analysis of Writing Tutorial Interactions between ESL Learners and Native-English Speaking Writing Center Tutors." PhD diss., Indiana University of Pennsylvania. ProQuest (AAT 3056649).

Ritter, Jennifer J., and Trygve Sandvik. 2009. "Meeting in the Middle: Bridging the Construction of Meaning with Generation 1.5 Learners." In *ESL writers: A Guide for Writing Center Tutors,* 2nd ed., edited by Shanti Bruce and Ben Rafoth. Portsmouth, NH: Boynton/Cook.

Sabatino, Lindsay, and Ben Rafoth. 2011. "World Englishes and Online Writing Centers." *International Journal of Innovation in English Language Teaching and Research* 1 (1): 1–11.

Sachs, Rebecca, and Charlene Polio. 2007. "Learners' Uses of Two Types of Written Feedback on an L2 Writing Revision Task." *Studies in Second Language Acquisition* 29 (01): 67–100. http://dx.doi.org/10.1017/S027226 3107070039.

Santa, Tracy. 2006. *Dead Letters: Error in Composition.* Creskill, NJ: Hampton.

Schmidt, Richard. 1994. "Deconstructing Consciousness in Search of Useful Definitions for Applied Linguistics." *AILA Review* 11:11–26.

Schwarzer, David, Melanie Bloom, and Sarah Shomo. 2006. *Research as a Tool for Empowerment: Theory Informing Practice.* Charlottesville, NC: Information Age.

Selinker, Larry. 1972. "Interlanguage." *International Review of Applied Linguistics* 10 (2): 209–31.

Severino, Carol, Shih-Ni Prim, Jane Cogie, and Lan Vu. 2013. "Analyzing Second Language (L2) Writing Problems & Tutors' Responses to Them." Paper presented at the Midwest Writing Centers Association conference, Chicago, IL., Nov. 1–3.

Shamoon, Linda K., and Deborah H. Burns. 1995. "A Critique of Pure Tutoring." *The Writing Center Journal* 15: 134–51.

Sharma, Yojana. 2012. "Fast Pace of Higher Education Enrollment Growth Predicted to Slow." University World News No. 213, March 13. http://www.universityworldnews.com/article.php?story=2012031308172724.

Shaughnessy, Mina. 1977. *Errors and Expectations.* New York: Oxford.

Sommers, Nancy, and Laura Saltz. 2004. "The Novice as Expert: Writing the Freshman Year." *College Composition and Communication* 56 (1): 124–49. http://dx.doi.org/10.2307/4140684.

Staben, Jennifer, and Kathryn Dempsey Nordhaus. 2009. "Looking at the Whole Text." In *ESL Writers: A Guide for Writing Center Tutors*, 2nd ed. Edited by Shanti Bruce and Ben Rafoth 78–90. Portsmouth, NH: Heinemann.

Swain, Merrill. 1985. "Communicative Competence: Some Roles of Comprehensible Input and Comprehensive Output in its Development." In *Input in Second Language Acquisition*, edited by Susan Gass and Carolyn G. Madden, 235–253. Rowley, MA: Newbury House.

Swain, Merrill. 2000. "The Output Hypothesis and Beyond: Mediating Acquisition through Collaborative Dialogue." In *Sociocultural Theory and Second Language Learning*, edited by James P. Lantolf, 97–114. Oxford, UK: Oxford University Press.

Swales, John M. 2001. "EAP-Related Linguistic Research: An Intellectual History." In *Research Perspectives on English for Academic Purposes*, edited by John Flowerdew and Matthew Peacock, 42–54. Cambridge, UK: Cambridge University Press. http://dx.doi.org/10.1017/CBO9781139524766.006.

Thaiss, Chris, Gerd Bräuer, Paula Carlino, Lisa Ganobcsik-Williams, and Aparna Sinha, eds. 2012. *Writing Programs Worldwide: Profiles of Academic Writing in Many Places*. Fort Collins, CO: WAC Clearinghouse.

Thaiss, Chris, and Terry Myers Zawacki. 2006. *Engaged Writers, Dynamic Disciplines: Research on the Academic Writing Life*. Portsmouth, NH: Boynton/Cook.

Thompson, Isabelle. 2009. "Scaffolding in the Writing Center: A Microanalysis of an Experienced Tutor's Verbal and Nonverbal Tutoring Strategies." *Written Communication* 26 (4): 417–53. http://dx.doi.org/10.1177/0741088309342364.

Thonney, Teresa. 2011. "Teaching the Conventions of Academic Discourse." *Teaching English in the Two Year College* 38 (4): 347–62.

Thonus, Terese. 2002. "Tutor and Student Assessments of Academic Writing Tutorials: What is 'Success'?" *Assessing Writing* 8 (2): 110–34. http://dx.doi.org/10.1016/S1075-2935(03)00002-3.

Thonus, Terese. 2004. "What Are the Differences? Tutor Interactions with First- and Second-Language Writers." *Journal of Second Language Writing* 13 (3): 227–42. http://dx.doi.org/10.1016/j.jslw.2004.04.012.

Thonus, Terese. 2012. "Corrective Language Feedback in L2 Writing Tutorials." Paper presented at the International Writing Centers Association conference, San Diego, CA.

Tokay, Dilek. 2012. "A Writing Center Journey at Sabanci University, Istanbul." In *Writing Programs Worldwide: Profiles of Academic Writing in Many Places*, edited by Chris Thaiss, Gerd Bräuer, Paula Carlino, Lisa Ganobcsik-Williams, and Aparna Sinha, 417–427. Fort Collins, CO: WAC Clearinghouse.

Toth, Barbara. 2012. "Announcing the PNU Writing Studio—And Our Journey toward *al itqan*." *MENAWCA Newsletter* (Spring): 7–8. http://menawca.org/7.html.

Trimbur, John. 2010. "Linguistic Memory and the Uneasy Settlement of U.S. English." In *Cross-Language Relations in Composition*, edited by Bruce Horner, Min-Zhan Lu, and Paul Kei Matsuda, 21–41. Carbondale: Southern Illinois University Press.

Truscott, John. 1996. "The Case against Grammar Correction in L2 Writing Classes." *Language Learning* 46 (2): 327–69. http://dx.doi.org/10.1111/j.1467-1770.1996.tb01238.x.

Truscott, John, and Angela Yi-Ping Hsu. 2008. "Error Correction, Revision, and Learning." *Journal of Second Language Writing* 17 (4): 292–305. http://dx.doi.org/10.1016/j.jslw.2008.05.003.

Valdés, Guadalupe. 1992. "Bilingual Minorities and Language Issues in Writing: Toward Professionwide Responses to a New Challenge." *Written Communication* 9 (1): 85–136. http://dx.doi.org/10.1177/0741088392009001003.

Webb, Stuart, and Michael. P. H. Rodgers. 2009a. "Vocabulary Demands of Television Programmes." *Language Learning* 59 (2): 335–66. http://dx.doi.org/10.1111/j.1467-9922.2009.00509.x.

Webb, Stuart, and Michael P. H. Rodgers. 2009b. "The Lexical Coverage of Movies." *Applied Linguistics* 30 (3): 407–27. http://dx.doi.org/10.1093/applin/amp010.

Wiener, Harvey S. 1986. "Collaborative Learning in the Classroom: A Guide to Evaluation." *College English* 48 (1): 52–61. http://dx.doi.org/10.2307/376586.

Williams, Jessica. 2008. "Tutoring L2 Writers: Insights from SLA Research." Paper presented at the International TESOL Convention, New York.

Williams, Jessica, and Carol Severino. 2004. "The Writing Center and Second Language Writers." *Journal of Second Language Writing* 13 (3): 165–72.

Wingate, Molly. 2005. "What Line? I Didn't See Any Line." In *A Tutor's Guide: Helping Writers One to One*, 2nd ed. Edited by Ben Rafoth, 9–16. Portsmouth, NH: Boynton/Cook.

Zamel, Vivian. 1997. "Toward a Model of Transculturation." *TESOL Quarterly* 31 (2): 341–52. http://dx.doi.org/10.2307/3588050.

ABOUT THE AUTHOR

BEN RAFOTH is Distinguished University Professor and director of the Writing Center at Indiana University of Pennsylvania, where he also teaches graduate courses in the composition and TESOL (teachers of English to speakers of other languages) program. Ben earned his master's in linguistics and doctorate in language education from the University of Georgia. He edited *A Tutor's Guide: Helping Writers One to One* and coedited, with Shanti Bruce, *ESL Writers: A Guide for Writing Center Tutors*, both in second editions. He served as an executive officer for the International Writing Centers Association and is a recipient of the Ron Maxwell Award from the National Conference on Peer Tutoring in Writing.

INDEX

Huang, Tung-chiou, 28
Hudson, R. A., 28
Hunter College, 58
Hutchison, Tom, 82
Hyland, Kenneth, 80, 82, 88–92

identities, 12, 37
idioms, 54, 118; idiomaticity, 43, 44,
    46
immersion, 56
immigrant, 33, 54–55
incomplete understanding, 62–63
India, 19, 124
Indiana University of Pennsylvania,
    60
input, 67–68, 128. *See also* compre-
    hensible: output
intended meaning, 94, 118
interaction, 40, 42, 49, 55, 79
interference, 106
interlanguage, 71, 106
International Research Foundation
    for English Language Education
    (IRFELE), 22
International Society for the
    Advancement of Writing Research
    (ISAWR), 22
international students, 21, 30–31, 33,
    49, 50, 56, 76, 126
International WAC/WID Mapping
    Project, 22
interviewing, 55
involvement, 86
Ioup, Georgette, 72
IRFELE. *See* International Research
    Foundation for English Language
    Education
Irvine, Patricia, 45
ISAWR. *See* International Society
    for the Advancement of Writing
    Research

Jackson, Frederic H., 124
Japan, 124
Japanese (language), 83
Jordon, Jay, 48, 124

Kail, Harvey, 35
Kenya, 124
King Abdulaziz University, 25

Kleifgen, Jo Anne, 29
Korea, 124
Krashen, Stephen, 67

language. *See by various names*
language acquisition, 41; learning,
    53. *See also* second-language
    acquisition
late-arriving resident, 30, 50, 118
Leki, Ilona, 83, 95–96, 126
Leung, Constant, 44
lexical knowledge, 75, 92–93, 108
Lightbown, Patsy M., 71, 106
linguistic: homogeneity, 48; variety,
    28
Linville, Cynthia, 110
listening, 38–39, 49, 51–52, 58
literacy, 52, 102
Liu, Pei-hsun Emma, 44–45
Lloyd, Marion, 20
Long, Michael, 48, 70
Lotbiniere, Max de, 56
Lu, Min-Zhan, 29, 48
Luxembourg, 124

Mackiewicz, Jo, 127
Malawi, 38
Malone, Margaret E., 124
Massey University, 23
Master, Peter, 82
Matsuda, Aya, 29–30
Matsuda, Paul Kei, 5, 16, 29–30, 38,
    47–48
McAndrew, Donald A., 108
McMurtrie, Beth, 21–22
meaning, 48
memorization, 67
MENAWCA. *See* Middle East-North
    Africa Writing Centers Alliance
metatalk, 126
metatext, 89–90, 117
Metcalf, Alan A., 32
Mexico, 20
Middle East-North Africa Writing
    Centers Alliance (MENAWCA),
    22, 37, 121
Mignolo, Walter D., 50
miscommunication, 14, 59, 66; misin-
    terpretation, 62–63, 65; misunder-
    standing, 59

modified interactions, 69–70, 112, 117; input, 70
monolingualism, 16, 54, 110, 136–38
motivation, 38, 43, 83
multilingual: tutors, 43, 99; writers, 39, 81, 85, 90, 126, 138
multilingualism, 23, 29, 54, 123. *See also* pluralingualism; translingualism

Nakamaru, Sarah, 95, 108
Nation, Paul, 76, 78–79
native-speaking tutors, 43–45
nativize, 45
negative transfer, 72
negotiated interaction, 8, 48, 63–65
Netherlands, the, 124, 130
Newkirk, Thomas, 126
Newton, Jonathan, 78–79
New Zealand, 124
Nigeria, 124
nominalizations, 92–94
nominative absolute, 93
nondirective tutoring, 5, 102
Nordhaus, Kathryn Dempsey, 102, 130
North, Stephen M., 132
Northwestern College, 25, 103
noticing, 106, 112–14, 117
Nova Southeastern University, 42, 51, 97

oral fluency, 49
output, 8; pushed, 68. *See also* comprehensible: output
overgeneralization, 106

patience, 66
Peirce, Bronwyn Norton, 45
Pelkowski, Stephanie, 102
Pennycook, Alastair, 102
Phillipson, Robert, 44
pluralingualism, 28. *See also* multilingualism; translingualism
Polio, Charlene, 111
Portuguese (language), 124
positive transfer, 72
Postcolonial Englishes, 45
postmodernism, 101–2
practice, 50

pragmatic, aspects of language, 50, 54, 108, 125
prepositions, 111
Princess Nora Bint Abdul Rahman University, 24, 35, 37
professionalization, 83
proficiency, 47, 54, 71
pronunciation, 43, 51
proofreading, 116

Qatar, 37

Rafoth, Ben, 44, 125
readability, 94
reading, 90
recasting, 8, 10–11, 46, 114, 117
reflections, 66
reformulation, 89–91
Reid, Joy, 50
Reigstad, Thomas J., 108
relationships, 42
research, 135
rewrite, 117
rhetorical choices, 94
Ritter, Jennifer, 49, 60, 63
Rodgers, Michael P. H., 76
Rowan, Karen, 12, 16
Russian (language), 124

Sabanci University, 23
Sabatino, Lindsay, 125
Sachs, Rebecca, 111
Saltz, Laura, 83–84
Sandvik, Trygve, 49
Santa, Tracy, 110
Saudi Arabia, 20, 35
scaffolding, 10, 65, 87, 130
Scardamalia, Marlene, 123
Schmidt, Richard, 112–13
Schwarzer, David, 29
second-language acquisition, 6, 73, 106, 126. *See also* language acquisition
Selinker, Larry, 71–72
semicolons, 113
Severino, Carol, 109
Shamoon, Linda K., 5
Sharma, Yojana, 19
Shaughnessy, Mina, 78, 106
Silva, Tony, 4